THOUGHT, WORDS AND CREATIVITY

Also by F. R. Leavis

★

FOR CONTINUITY
NEW BEARINGS IN ENGLISH POETRY
REVALUATION
EDUCATION AND THE UNIVERSITY
THE GREAT TRADITION
THE COMMON PURSUIT
D. H. LAWRENCE: NOVELIST
'ANNA KARENINA' AND OTHER ESSAYS
ENGLISH LITERATURE IN OUR TIME AND
THE UNIVERSITY
NOR SHALL MY SWORD
THE LIVING PRINCIPLE

with Q. D. Leavis
LECTURES IN AMERICA
DICKENS THE NOVELIST

with Michael Yudkin
TWO CULTURES?

with Denys Thompson
CULTURE AND ENVIRONMENT

Edited by F. R. Leavis
DETERMINATIONS
MILL ON BENTHAM AND COLERIDGE

Edited by John Tasker
LETTERS IN CRITICISM

Thought, Words and Creativity
ART AND THOUGHT IN LAWRENCE

By

F. R. LEAVIS

1976

CHATTO & WINDUS

LONDON

Published by
Chatto & Windus Ltd
40 William IV Street
London WC2N 4DF

★

Clarke, Irwin & Co.,
Toronto

ISBN 0 7011 2182 3

© F. R. Leavis 1976

Printed in Great Britain by
Cox & Wyman Ltd
London, Fakenham and Reading

CONTENTS

*It is not the fact of judging rightly or wrongly –
truth is not within our reach – but the lack of
scruple which makes them omit the elementary
requirements for right judgment.*

ORTEGA Y GASSET *The Revolt of the Masses*

*Such a result is the logical outcome of Professor
Myrdal's conception of man and society. By
decrying cultural, ethnic, religious and economic
differences, and unceasingly inveighing against
discrimination, he seeks to build a society which
is profoundly dehumanised.*

P. T. BAUER *Dissent on Development*

*Man or woman, each is a flow, a flowing life.
And without one another, we can't flow, just as a
river cannot flow without banks. A woman is one
bank of the river of my life, and the world is the
other.*

D. H. LAWRENCE

ACKNOWLEDGEMENTS

The author and publisher would like to thank the following for permission to quote from the works of D. H. Lawrence:

Laurence Pollinger Ltd., William Heinemann Ltd. and the Estate of the late Mrs. Frieda Lawrence. The Viking Press, Inc., New York for excerpts from: *The Captain's Doll*, Copyright © 1923 by Thomas B. Seltzer, Inc., Copyright renewed 1951 by Frieda Lawrence; *Women In Love*, Copyright © 1920, 1922 by D. H. Lawrence, Copyright renewed 1948, 1950 by Frieda Lawrence; *The Rainbow*, Copyright © 1915 by D. H. Lawrence, Copyright renewed 1943 by Frieda Lawrence; *Fantasia of the Unconscious*, Copyright © 1922 by Thomas B. Seltzer, Inc., Copyright renewed 1950 by Frieda Lawrence; *Psychoanalysis and the Unconscious*, Copyright © 1921 by Thomas B. Seltzer, Inc., Copyright renewed 1949 by Frieda Lawrence; *The Fox*, Copyright © 1923 by Thomas B. Seltzer, Inc., Copyright renewed 1951 by Frieda Lawrence; *Phoenix I*, Copyright © 1936 by Frieda Lawrence, Copyright renewed 1964 by the Estate of the late Frieda Lawrence Ravagli. All rights reserved. *Phoenix II*, Copyright © 1959, 1963, 1968 by the Estate of Frieda Lawrence Ravagli. All rights reserved. *The Collected Letters of D. H. Lawrence*, Copyright © 1962 by Angelo Ravagli and C. M. Weekley, Executors of the Estate of Frieda Lawrence Ravagli. All rights reserved. Alfred Knopf, Inc., New York, for excerpts from *The Plumed Serpent* and *Mornings in Mexico*.

PREFACE

IT OCCURRED to me to say that, but for an emphasis on the word 'thought', my commentaries on the works of Lawrence I examine in the following book don't differ from the critiques that I should have written without the special purpose that the emphasis represents. But I pulled myself up, realizing that such a statement would be misleading. For one thing, the special purpose entails a special, and a restricted, choice of works to be closely examined, and the criteria that govern the choice lead to differences of treatment that go with the restriction. No intelligent critic would aspire to include in his written critique all the considerations that occur to him on his way to what he feels to be a just appreciation of a major novel or *nouvelle*: the attempt to be exhaustive would exhaust or bore the reader. The critic must have his own approach and a selective line of discourse, and my selection and line are affected by the special purpose they serve.

The nature of my approach in this book is made plain in the first chapter, and in justifying and enforcing the considerations that form my argument there I aim at a certain economy—indeed the force of the total argument depends on that. Of course, some repetition is necessary, but the due enforcement involves variation in the embodiment of the thought, for the variation means a different context of developments and connections—I am thinking of the embracing organic totality of Lawrence's thought. One must choose works which bear a convenient relation to one another—convenient as furthering adequacy as well as economy. So the choice isn't altogether easy.

I deal mainly with four works: *The Plumed Serpent*, *Women in Love*, *The Captain's Doll* and *The Rainbow*—in that order. Though Lawrence himself judged *The Plumed Serpent*, at any rate when he had first finished the writing of it, to be the 'most important thing he had done so far', I don't hesitate to consider it largely—and consciously—as a foil to *Women in Love*, which I am not alone in judging the greatest and most important of his novels. I don't go on to consider next *The Rainbow*, to which in any case Lawrence called *Women in Love* a sequel—as it is. I find the discursive exposition of Lawrence's art as thought is best served by going on to deal with *The Captain's Doll*, which is one of his supreme *nouvelles*. Before deciding that, I gave a glance towards that other of the supreme *nouvelles*, *St Mawr*, but rejected that choice because it didn't, as *The Captain's Doll* did, lend itself to the development of my exposition in the way I saw before me. I couldn't, given my emphasis on 'thought' and the accompanying need for economy, think of trying to exemplify the astonishing variety in mode—in tone or *timbre*— that characterizes Lawrence's great masterpieces that present themselves as tales. While *St Mawr* occupies the greater part of the volume called that, *The Captain's Doll*, which is also long, and much more like a novel than the work that accompanied it, appeared first in a volume to which the other tale gave its title: *The Ladybird*.

Seeing what it undertakes to do, *The Ladybird* is a surprising success. One tone prevails in it, an ominous solemnity associated with the horror of the war, and its theme is escape from the unsatisfyingness, the unreality, of idealizing, 'perfect' love. Nothing could well be a greater contrast than that tale to *The Captain's Doll*, which, among the diversities of its shifting tone, is always profoundly serious, but never solemn. The passage backwards and forwards for comparative reference between *The Captain's Doll* and *Women in Love* is easy and natural, but the menace at the heart of the novel—it has a quasi-cosmic effect on us—is absent in the tale.

I gave up the idea of discussing in detail *The Fox* as a whole; it proved unnecessary. I have used *The Fox* to make the comparisons that helped me in my attempt to elicit from such of Lawrence's 'art-speech' as I do consider closely a not too crude idea of Lawrence's thought, and what I found helpful about the tale was that its significances were likely to be clear enough to any real reader of Lawrence in any case: it was sufficient to refer articulately to certain of them in relation to texts I examine carefully as wholes.

My fifth chapter is called 'The Rainbow', and is devoted to the novel with that title. I have dealt with *The Rainbow* after

PREFACE

the 'sequel' because *Women in Love* is a self-sufficient great novel.
Nevertheless *The Rainbow* is far from irrelevant to it; the 'historical' background brings out the significance of the 'sequel' —
notably the element of paradox at the heart of *Women in Love*;
paradox that is inseparable from his greatness, conditions it,
and makes him so important to us. I have found it impossible
to deal with the meaning, the communication, that gives form
to *The Rainbow* except in terms of the paradox — which the title
and the insistence on the rainbow-symbol in the text are so clearly
meant to bring home to us.

As I point out in the chapter, the emergence of the Brangwens
from their immemorial rustic traditionalism towards the possibility of the Eastwood intelligentsia and its cultural milieu, of
which Lawrence was the inspiring centre and on which his
genius fed, was at the same time the development of the civilization that produced industrialized Eastwood. He had no thought
of reconciling the human potentiality in himself to an arrest at
what is represented by Tom Brangwen — nor had Tom Brangwen,
who married the Polish lady, himself. That would have been
anti-human and anti-life.

Lawrence is quite clear with himself about this; that is, he
recognizes the paradox to which he commits himself. I have
quoted below[1] as part of a longer quotation the following:

So there has been produced machinery, to take the place of the
human machine. And the inventor of the labour-saving machine has
been hailed as a public benefactor, and we have rejoiced over his
discovery. Now there is a railing against the machine as if it were an
evil thing. And the thinkers talk about the return to the mediaeval
system of handicrafts. Which is absurd.

But the machine means industrialism, and industrialism produces
industrialized Eastwood. Lawrence throws out, for the given
context, an implicit definition of 'work' in 'machinery to take
the place of the human machine'. He is well aware that there are
menacing human problems involved here. In *Women in Love*
Gerald, the modernizer of the Crich mines, killed the pleasure
in life, the satisfaction, the men had found in their work

[1] See page 150 below. The quoted passage comes from *Study of Thomas
Hardy*, *Phoenix I*, page 426. An extensive context would repay *ad hoc* re-
reading.

underground, and they hated him for it. He killed it by making them conscious of being slaves of machinery—something too like 'human machines'. In the same novel (page 448), Loerke, offering to substantiate his proposition that 'Art should interpret industry, as art once interpreted religion', replies to Gudrun's doubting question about the 'great granite frieze':

'Certainly. What is man doing, when he is at a fair like this? He is fulfilling the counterpart of labour—the machine works him instead of he the machine. He enjoys the mechanical motion in his own body.'

I adduce Loerke, not as a dramatic voice of Lawrence's thought, but as evidencing that thought grappling with the problem of what work means in industrial society in relation to art, being and culture. When, in 1930, Lawrence died, the stupefying and inhuman boredom of service in the assembly-line was not, for critics of modern civilization, quite the commonplace as representative of industrialism it was soon to become. But to the greater number of persons employed in industry their work hadn't the human significance that could give it—beyond their wages—what could bring them satisfaction. There is little wonder that the unions devoted their efforts, with success, to forcing wages up and hours of work down. I have commented on the change represented by the triumph, even in *Times* leaders, of 'job' and 'joblessness' over 'employment' and 'unemployment'. Every 'worker', the government knows, is entitled to a job, and a job is primarily the right to wages. I needn't go into here the other advantages conferred on industrial workers by the victory of the trade-unions.

But the workers—like, in fact, most of the population—are disinherited; they share the confident materialism of a technologico-Benthamite civilization (though the confidence is departing). The small minority who know that money, 'welfare', 'democracy', and spiritual philistinism can't bring satisfaction or save civilization from collapse are faced with a problem. It's the problem that Lawrence saw as insoluble when he said (I quote from the epigraph to *The Living Principle* taken from him):

It is no use trying merely to modify present forms. The whole great form of our era will have to go. And nothing will really send it down but the new shoots of life springing up and slowly bursting the foundations. And one can do nothing but fight tooth and nail to defend the new shoots of life from being crushed out, and let them grow.

I pointed out that Lawrence can hardly be said to have done nothing. My whole assumption in this book and in *The Living Principle* is that we find we *have* to do all we can. In fact, though things are so much worse than they were in Lawrence's life-time, our attitude—our inevitable attitude—is not essentially different from what I discuss as the paradox of his in my chapter on *The Rainbow*. We cannot act as if the smash were certain to come, and very soon; our business is to watch for fresh shoots to defend. It seems probable that after a smash there would be no shoots, and that the possibility of them, at any rate for a very long time, would be destroyed in blood, famine, fire and detonations.

We have to assume that our civilization will go on. It depends on an economic basis that we shouldn't dare to destroy if we could. The economic dependence generates a habit, which has become second nature, of technologico-Benthamite philistinism. Even the absorption of women on a large scale into industry and affairs that is so grave a menace to *humanitas* will have to go on— in any case, for a long time: otherwise the economy, the whole complex machine of civilization, would break down, with unmanageable consequences.

No life at all is likely to issue out of total catastrophe. We have to go on practising our firmly centred, our rooted opportunisms. The faith that we must keep alive is that what we stand for *are* the living shoots. Lawrence—and not the less for what I have called the 'paradox'—is a potent inspiration and source of strength to that end.

There was indeed felicity in making *The Rainbow*, of those chosen, the final text to be discussed.

THOUGHT, WORDS AND CREATIVITY

L'INTELLIGENCE is not the same as intelligence: how often have I found myself telling students that! Of course, I may be said to take a liberty when I commit myself to such a statement, not being able to point to any authority for it in the dictionaries. But the English language permits—even encourages —the user to take these liberties, as the French language doesn't. The force and justice of my opening would be brought out in any intelligent study of D. H. Lawrence. What 'intelligent' means here is what Lawrence compels the perceptive reader to recognize. To say this is to pay his genius a due tribute, and to insist on his importance to us in the present human crisis.

Yet Eliot in the 'thirties, intending pretty obviously a severe adverse judgment on anything offered as Laurentian thought, wrote somewhere (I think it was in *The Criterion*), that Lawrence was 'incapable of what is ordinarily called thinking'. It is true that Eliot in his later life, after he had abandoned poetry for the series of theatre-plays that opens so disconcertingly with *The Cocktail Party*, said that of course he had changed his mind about Lawrence since those days. But he said nothing, so far as I know, to suggest that he recognized astonishing powers, so profound and compelling, of original thought in Lawrence—powers that belonged with his creativity. Compelling?—Eliot was not alone in *not* being compelled: our civilization breeds blankness to the wonder and significance of the creativity.

Eliot himself was a distinguished creative writer, but there is striking paradox in that: the fact that the genius appears only in a very limited way in the criticism is a manifestation of the paradox. Lawrence's criticism has had practically no attention at all, but Eliot as critic has a very high conventional standing. The nature of the convention is suggested by this, which I find in a review by Professor W. W. Robson of which a cutting (from *The Times Higher Educational Supplement*) has just been sent me:

> Leavis's originality is harder to specify than Empson's. Perhaps it may be said that his best discussions combine an Empsonian attention to verbal detail with Eliot's capacity to see the wood for the trees.

I'll not comment on the assimilation of me to Empson; my concern is with the manner and implication of the reference, which isn't after all very neat, to Eliot. What the formulation implicitly does, or intends to do, is to lay the emphasis on his critical intelligence. And indeed his accepted standing is that of a great critic. Actually his good criticism is virtually confined to places immediately relevant to the work of the 'practitioner' (significantly Eliot's word) who, as the 1914 war drew to a close, 'altered expression' (his own phrase), and proved that something *could* happen in English poetry after Swinburne. His range of real firsthand judgment was extremely limited, and the highly esteemed and characteristic 'Tradition and the Individual Talent' is only speciously distinguished, not merely marked stylistically as it is by affectation, but pretentiously null as thought.

It represents the Francophilia he had contracted at Harvard. A striking manifestation of this is to be seen in the confident pronouncement that the important thing is that France had a mature prose before England. Though commonly believed, it's simply not true—if 'mature' means 'modern' in the sense defined by what Sprat records of the Royal Society's requirement regarding the prose in which communications were to be written. But the essential retort runs: 'The important thing surely is that we had our Shakespeare half-a-dozen decades before France had her Racine—by when the great change in civilization had been consummated.'

One sees that Eliot had an uncritical admiration for Valéry's 'brilliant' prose: the French exhibitionistic aplomb that constitutes Valéry's brilliance clearly influenced him. I myself admired 'Le Cimetière Marin' (in too unqualified a way, I now realize) in the 1920s, but I found I had no use for Valéry's prose—unless to examine paragraphs of it with my pupils as exemplifying the confusions, vacuities, and non-sequiturs that a training in *la clarté* and *la logique* didn't exclude. I used a good deal, I remember, a Valerian piece that appeared first in *La Nouvelle Revue Française*: 'Préface à un Commentaire', the commentary being an interpretive offer that Alain had written on 'Le Cimetière Marin', in front of which it was to be printed in a special edition. I still have, bought in 1924 when it came out *à tirage restreint*, published by Cobden-Sanderson 'For *The Criterion*', a little book containing 'Le Serpent' (Valéry's 'Ébauche d'un Serpent'—the French text with a translation *en regard*) together with an introductory essay by Eliot. The essay exemplifies Eliot's exasperating Francophil mannerisms: exhibitionism, false aplomb and fallacious suggestion; in sum, the intellectual feebleness that has commonly passed for brilliance. This is representative:

> To English amateurs, rather inclined to dismiss poetry which appears reticent, and to peer lasciviously between the lines for biographical confession, such an activity may appear no better than a *jeu de quilles*. But Boileau was a fine poet, and he spoke in seriousness. To reduce one's disorderly and mostly silly personality to the gravity of a *jeu de quilles* would be to do an excellent thing: yet for this a great poet, Landor, has been condemned to obloquy. . . . One is prepared for art when one has ceased to be interested in one's own emotions and experiences except as material . . . .

There is no more to Eliot's famous doctrine of Impersonality than this. But he was of course himself a poet of genius, and in 1924 he could hardly, had he been as capable of thought as he supposed, have offered his critical doctrine as throwing much light on the genesis, nature and distinction of his own poetry. As for his most impressive work, which, from *Ash-Wednesday* on, enacts a religious quest, Eliot could hardly have said in response to the challenge: yes, he *was* offering this as poetry fairly describable as a *jeu de quilles*. But, though those early 'theoretical' utterances have become 'classical', he wrote, or at any rate published, nothing to correct or question the doctrine they asserted. This, however, is not the main point, which is that, while his magnum opus, *Four Quartets*, is devoted to sustained exploratory thought, the thought frustrates itself by reason of the contradiction at its heart: seeking to establish an apprehension of the supremely Real, source of 'spiritual' values, by the use of his gifts as a poet—

by (that is) his creative art in using the English language, he denies human creativity. It is reasonable to say that our all-conquering civilization has killed the very idea of creativity—and *not* in the interest of spiritual values. Its ethos at any rate is an implicit denial of the vitally creative.

In its sudden loss of confidence, its glimpse of newly imaginable disaster, it—in politicians of all parties, *Times* leaders, the voices of the eminent wise, (Sir Keith Joseph brackets with Mr Cecil King as the kind of exception we have to expect)—talks merely of how to restore a steady rate of economic growth and a constantly rising standard of living (a matter of money to buy things with and a sure and growing supply of things to buy). It can't really believe in the menace hanging over it; it is incapable of grasping the patent diagnostic truth, so rapid has progress been, so stupefying the effect on human life of the continuous industrial revolution, which is constantly accelerating, and of the science that breeds the progress.

For Eliot, of course, this civilization is the Waste Land, and if we still had an influential educated public he, as the impressive witness he is, would be—would so far be—a power to be invoked by defenders of humanity. But there is the paradox: in offering to expose and transcend with his creative 'logic' the neo-Benthamite world's spiritual philistinism, he explicitly, as an indisputable premise, himself denies human creativity. The denial entails the self-contradiction that emasculates his thought, depriving it of all the cogency intended. The inner personal pressures behind the supremely difficult enterprise of thought defeat it—this is the irony of the 'case' Eliot never ceases to be. He doesn't himself recognize the defeat; it is a defeat of intelligence.

Eliot matters in a major way because he is impressive enough as a creative writer to bring out by contrast the greatness and rarity of the genius who was *not* defeated—who demonstrates so marvellously what intelligence is. No one of course who has *read* him would suggest that Lawrence doesn't bring home to us that it is an essential condition of life-as-intelligence to know itself faced—ultimately, but not remotely—with the unknown, and with the unknowable. Lawrence's awareness of the unknown and the unknowable, however, unlike Eliot's, is at the same time an exaltation of creative life, and inseparable from an acceptance of responsibility as inhering, necessarily, in the human individual's self-gathered, delicately intent and unanalysably intuitive wholeness.

But I mustn't be trapped into developing further the contrast between the two differently distinguished writers. I have said enough for my purpose, which is focused on Lawrence. I can only, with any brevity, suggest the nature of my focal concern by saying that it regards thought, art and language. I have reminded you of Eliot's unfavourable view of Lawrence's capacity for thought. I have told you of my own adversely critical judgment on Eliot's own intellectual prose, and have associated its fallacious 'brilliance' with his Francophilia. Certainly no one who admired Valéry, the critic as well as the poet, in so unreserved a way could be expected to conceive it an urgent matter to achieve some currency for a more intelligent conception of intelligence than that actually prevailing in Bloomsbury. I have made it plain, I hope, that in predicating 'brilliance' of 'Tradition and the Individual Talent' and the like Eliotic performances I mean shallowness; and I think I justified the charge when, at the University of Bristol some time ago, I quoted from one of his more valuable critiques the passage in which he laments that Blake insisted on creating (Eliot's word) his own philosophy instead of taking over—as Dante did—one ready-made, and concentrating on what really concerned the poet: the poetry. It is characteristic of Eliot in his criticism to use the word 'poetry' in that quasi-absolute way—a way that is implied in his habit of calling himself a 'practitioner'. Actually his art never *was* for him a mere craft-skill, an art of playing skittles, and in *Four Quartets* it is very apparent that he is not only dealing without disguise with the pressure of intense personal need, but consciously and unequivocally identifies the art with the very process of thought—thought that the pressure generates in order to clarify itself. That clarification doesn't ensue is due to the pressure's being pathological and causing blindness that intelligence in Eliot can't overcome. No creative writer of the greatest kind is a 'case', but Eliot remained one to the end.

Lawrence, like Dickens (*pace* the late Edmund Wilson, who made *him* a 'case'), *was* a creative writer of the greatest kind, and though he died in 1930, he is essentially of our time: the

19

civilization he diagnosed is ours. The changes of the last half-century have unnervingly borne out the diagnosis. Since we have him (though we ignore him) my theme is the less merely theoretical. I will indicate its nature, virtually quoting from my most recent book.

Three propositions or constatations, serve to convey what the theme is:

(1) There could be no developed thought of the most important kind without language.

(2) Our language is English, which has a great literature, so that one had better say: the completest use of the English language is to be found in major creative works.

(3) A major creative writer *knows* that in composing and writing a major creative work his concern is to refine and develop his profounder thought about life (the concluding three-word phrase unambiguously eliminates mathematics).

Eliot in his paradoxical way is a highly distinguished poet, and should be seen as being of decided importance to us today; but Lawrence is a far greater creative power. There is in *him* no basic contradiction. In his varied, voluminous and wide-ranging *oeuvre*, his concern is always with developing a sense of what vital intelligence is, and this entails a conception of art and of the relation of art to thought very different from that implied (if anything to be called a conception *is*) in Eliot's relevant utterances. To Lawrence the notion of thought as something apart from the creative writer's creativity in the way suggested by Eliot's censure on Blake would have been absurd. *His* thought wasn't separable from his art, which it could never occur to him to call a game of skittles. True, we have to distinguish, with his *oeuvre* in front of us, between what challenges us to read it as completely achieved art (*Women in Love, The Fox, The Captain's Doll*) and what unmistakably offers us something else (*The Crown, Study of Thomas Hardy, Psychoanalysis and the Unconscious*).

These last three, which I have grouped together for the immediate purpose, differ markedly among themselves in mode and method, but the Laurentian creative writer is essentially present in them all. The last, *Psychoanalysis and the Unconscious*, is the one of the three to invoke in exposing the absurdity of Eliot's privative judgment on Lawrence that denies him all capacity for developed thought.

The book, which starts off as a refutation of Freud's incest-doctrine, never, though it deals with the profoundest and most difficult of problems, ceases to hold the reader as a sustained piece of cogent exposition. One can quote passage after passage so firm and supple in its logic that it makes Eliot's rash pronouncement look distinctly questionable. Two or three pages read on end dispose of Eliot's wisdom as the prejudiced irresponsibility it is. The purpose of the book isn't negative; Lawrence's aim is to enforce his criticism of our civilization and culture by showing what the human individual in his wholeness, his living integrity as the actual presence of life, must be realized to be. And to succeed in that is to exemplify what vital intelligence is—the intelligence needed for valid thought about life.

The undertaking is difficult and delicate in that the mental consciousness plays, and *must* play, an essential part in it—the mental consciousness from its disastrous misconceived trust in which Lawrence would like to rescue civilized humanity. 'The mind,' he says, 'as author and director of life is anathema.' But he also says:

True, we must all develop into mental consciousness. But mental consciousness is not a goal; it is a cul-de-sac. It provides us only with endless appliances for the all-too-difficult business of coming to our spontaneous-creative fulness of being.

Mental consciousness is inevitably involved in Lawrence's thought, which is so intimately preoccupied with that 'all-too-difficult business'. The thought itself (which *is* thought) of *Psychoanalysis and the Unconscious*, therefore, is in a sense difficult in its delicacy, which is extreme, seeing how readily mind falls into aberrations, into illusions about itself, its function, its authority and its powers—how ego and will take it over and cut it off from the source of spontaneity. Lawrence finds that Freud of the incest-theory has fallen victim to a subtly besetting danger of mental consciousness. The Laurentian 'hunting down' of the pristine, the primal unconscious was impelled by the need to to expose unanswerably the error of that Freudian doctrine. Lawrence has to use thought in enforcing his criticism, which is basic, of Freud's thought, and the enforcement entails an account of the nature and conditions of the vital intelligence out of which all valid thought must issue.

The clear expository efficiency of the argument means that you are conscious all the while of D. H. Lawrence expounding. And this is so of all the pieces that don't claim to be what you wouldn't take them to be: the art that has the fully impersonal and complete createdness implied by the word 'art' when used in that sense. The prose in which they are written is felt to be, as between the inclusive extremes represented by *Psychoanalysis and the Unconscious* and *The Crown*, in varying degrees expository —even when evocative and hortatory as well. What varies with the different modes is the reader's sense of a gap between the verbal presentation of the directed thought and that on which the thought is directed. In the art the felt separation between the creatively used words and the piece of living they have the function of evoking is at a minimum. One is not kept conscious of Lawrence—not kept actively aware of him as a personal voice expounding or aiming to evoke. And he, when he feels that he has got his art right, is hardly conscious of any gap. He is realizing in imagination a completely (or purely) 'significant' piece of living: yet he is himself, in his integrity as an individual being, present in the work. This is the true impersonality; it is of supreme importance to any conception of what the essential, fully imagined, spiritual status or stance or human reality (perhaps all three nouns are needed) might achieve. The impersonality that Eliot credits Landor or Valéry with is idea and emptiness in the one case, and mere French brilliance and aplomb on the other.

But Lawrence was so fully conscious that there could be no originative priority as thought ascribable either to *Women in Love* on the one hand or to *Psychoanalysis and the Unconscious* on the other—they derive in perfect directness from the one vital intelligence and the one achieved wholeness of individual being—that he played with the notion expressed here:

Plato's Dialogues are queer little novels. It seems to me that it was the greatest pity in the world, when philosophy and fiction got split. They used to be one, right from the days of myth. Then they went and parted, like a nagging married couple, with Aristotle and Thomas Aquinas and that beastly Kant. So the novel went sloppy, and philosophy went abstract-dry. The two should come together again—in the novel.

What is at issue is the nature of thinking; Lawrence is expressing his distaste for the kind of intellectuality that starts, as so much philosophical writing does, from a mathematico-logical assumption about the criteria of valid thought, and can't escape from them. It remains blankly unaware that they certainly don't apply—frustratingly don't—in fields where a full vital intelligence, with its suppleness and delicacy, is essential. And it is not only philosophy, and not only French thought—thought about life, that suffer from the Cartesian heritage. I've noted in my last book, how Stanislas Andreski in *Social Sciences as Sorcery* had incurred seriously disabling weaknesses by his naïvety about the nature of language, and so about the nature of intelligence and thought, and how he assumed with innocent confidence that he might cite Russell's logic as final on 'fact and value'.

What accounts for such confidence is not, I think, any close study of Russell, but a routine conception of sound thought as controlled by *la clarté* and *la logique*—by criteria not essentially at odds with what those French words suggest.

'Logic', says Lawrence, 'is far too coarse to make the subtle distinctions life demands'. That is not a specious plea for licentious irresponsibility. In *Fantasia of the Unconscious* we read: 'Only by fine delicate knowledge can we recognize and release our impulses'. Lawrence is insisting that thought, which necessarily involves mental consciousness, is indispensable. But he insists at the same time that the thought demanded by life is not an affair of mental consciousness alone—or rather that vital mental consciousness is neither apart in the individual human being, separated off, nor dominating, initiating and controlling.

I must revert here to the criticism Lawrence brings in *Psychoanalysis and the Unconscious* against Freud's incest-theory. He finds himself challenged to 'hunt down' the 'pristine unconscious':

We have actually to go back to our own unconscious. But not to the unconscious which is the inverted reflection of our ideal consciousness. ['Ideal' here refers directly to 'idea', that which belongs to the mind.] We must discover, if we can, the true unconscious where our life bubbles up in us, prior to our mentality. The first bubbling life in us, which is innocent of any mental alteration, this is the unconscious. It is the spontaneous origin from which it behoves us to live.

What then is the true unconscious? It is not a shadow cast by the mind. It is the spontaneous life-motive in every organism. Where does it begin? It begins where life begins. But that is too vague. It is no use talking about life and the unconscious in bulk. You can talk about electricity, because electricity is a homogeneous force, conceivable apart from any incorporation. But life is inconceivable as a general thing. It exists only in living creatures. So that life begins, now as always, in an individual living creature. In the beginning of the individual living creature is the beginning of life, every time and always, and life has no beginning apart from this.

Lawrence is making, for his purpose, the point that I for mine make when I say that '"life" is a necessary word, but life is "there" only in the individual being.' *His* insistence runs:

Where the individual begins, life begins. The two are inseparable, life and individuality. And also, where the individual begins, the unconscious, which is the specific life-motive, also begins.

The emphasis falls for my own purpose on what I call the Third Realm (neither private nor, for science, public), which both my purpose and my firm certitude represent by language, in which, having created it, individuals meet, and in meeting (they meet in meaning) carry on the creative collaboration that maintains and renews what we think of as a life—i.e. the language. But this 'life' (inverted commas now—though it's a reality and a key one) couldn't exist but for the life that's 'there' only in individuals (and human individuals couldn't live without that non-computerable reality).

Lawrence in *Psychoanalysis and the Unconscious* traces the development that starts with conception to the arrival at completed individuality in the mature human being: 'At the moment of conception, when a procreative male nucleus fuses with the nucleus of the female germ, at that moment does a new unit of life arise in the universe.' There would be no point in my trying to write a précis of the account Lawrence gives in terms of a growing complexity of polarities between centres within the new individual, accompanied first by essential polarities between the foetus and the mother who carries it in her womb; accompanied and complicated later by a play of polarities involving not only the mother, but other individuals external to the individual child: the thing is done so lucidly and convincingly by Lawrence in his quite short book.

It will be plain to any reader that Lawrence owes in an essential way to specialists he has read; but it will be plain also that he has read with an intelligence creatively quick to take hints in the way it judges them worth taking, and that its judgment is supremely responsible. That astonishing power of thought in acquiring and using knowledge got from books is an aspect of his living genius.

I have dwelt deliberately on the word 'thought', so essential to my undertaking—used it again and again in characterizing Lawrence's creativity. *Psychoanalysis and the Unconscious* is unmistakably a remarkable product of thought. This emphasis, repeated challengingly in these last sentences, might seem to be at odds with what he writes in (for example) the opening of chapter III of *Fantasia of the Unconscious*:

> The primal consciousness in man is pre-mental, and has nothing to do with cognition. It is the same as in the animals. And this pre-mental-consciousness remains, as long as we live, the powerful root and body of our consciousness. The mind is but the last flower, the *cul de sac*. . . . Thought, let us say what we will about its magic powers, is instrumental only, the soul's finest instrument for the business of living. Thought is just a means to action and living. But life and action take rise actually at the great centres of dynamic consciousness. The solar plexus, the greatest and most important centre of our dynamic consciousness, is a sympathetic centre. At this great centre of our first-mind we know as we can never mentally know. Primarily we know, each man, each living creature knows, profoundly and satisfactorily and without question, that *I am I*. This root of all knowledge and being is established at the solar plexus; it is dynamic, pre-mental knowledge, such as cannot be transferred into thought. Do not ask me to transfer the pre-mental dynamic knowledge into thought. It cannot be done. The knowledge that *I am I* can never be thought: only known. This being the very first term of our life-knowledge, a knowledge established physically and psychically . . . .

Some comment is needed. Thought serves the soul so well as its finest instrument because it can be so much more, its relation to living from 'the root and body of our consciousness' so other, than what the word 'instrument' suggests. Lawrence knows this, having exemplified in his *oeuvre* the inescapable truth of it. What he warns us against are the insidious dangers that attend on being mentally conscious; what he inveighs against is the misuse of the mind that makes it an enemy of life. He exposes and inveighs a great deal, because that misuse is the distinctive mark of our scientifico-industrial civilization. To the malady that results he applies diagnostically the triad, 'will, ego and idea'. The will is that of the closed ego—Blake's 'selfhood' as distinguished from the 'identity', and the triad of terms together means the mind, the mental consciousness, offering to work life according to its ideas, which, with the mental consciousness they belong to, have been cut off from the well-head and from the centres of living power.

It is with thought, lived and living thought—for there is nothing else to resort to, that Lawrence sets about rescuing life from this inner mechanization. Not merely of *Psychoanalysis and the Unconscious*, but of any one of his novels we can say that it is a searching of experience in the concrete 'knowledge', not only of the desired individual wholeness, but of what 'spontaneity' means and, with it, 'responsibility'. The knowledge that *I am I* can never be thought: 'only known'—that is a separable statement of Lawrence's. We needn't question it; but it doesn't mean that such knowledge can't *tell* appropriately in living thought: it does so—that is, is effectively present—in the thought that Lawrence communicates (expression and making communicable are one).

When he brings out the pronouncement about the knowledge that *I am I* he is insisting on the fact—basically indisputable, but not readily graspable in a world of mass-democracy, statistical truths, and computers that can write poems—that life is not a force like electricity: it is in the concrete actuality always an individual, and if treated as if it could be made general, ceases to be there. My own formulation of that truth invokes the nature of language: individuals alone can mean, but they mean in order to meet and commune in meaning. Not only does the individual *need* relations with others, but the vital relations are creative—and creative of a reality that transcends language.

Without the English language waiting quick and ready for him,

Lawrence couldn't have communicated his thought: that is obvious enough. But it is also the case that he couldn't have thought it. English as he found it was a product of an immemorial *sui generis* collaboration on the part of its speakers and writers. It is alive with promptings and potentialities, and the great creative writer shows his genius in the way he responds. Any writer of the language must depend on what his readers know already (though they may not know that they know) — must evoke it with the required degree of sharpness or latency. Lawrence, doing that, faces the problem of evoking the appropriate stir or glimmer of the kind of knowledge of which he himself has said that it can't be thought, but only known—faces it triumphantly. He can establish a specificity of imagined experience out of which the apprehension flashes on the reader, or makes its presence felt as an implicit intuition: in any case appropriately.

A specificity of imagined experience—'imagination', like all important words, has a number of values: Lawrence's thought, which is inseparable from his major creativity, gives it one that has a profoundly Laurentian potency and resonance. I mustn't try to say more about it now. I will at the moment merely, by way of enforcing my point, quote again this: 'At the maximum of our imagination we are religious.' I can't think of anyone but Lawrence from whom that could have come.

'Imagination' isn't, in Lawrence's thought and expository 'logic', the only term of major importance that doesn't, as it stands alone, sufficiently explain itself—doesn't define or reveal its value in a brief quoted passage. It might, for instance, be said that, in the Laurentian sentence I have just separated from all the context it actually implies, 'religious' needs even more than 'imagination' to have its value defined or specified. But it is the word 'life' that faces Laurentian thought with its most formidable problem—or rather, troubles most the expositor of Laurentian thought. 'The knowledge that *I am I*' necessarily carries with it the knowledge that *I am alive*. The predicate here imputes life, but the implied word 'life' isn't charged with the value it has in the Laurentian dictum: 'Nothing is important but life.' This dictum, pondered, will perhaps be felt to be a complex or telescoping proposition. Nevertheless, those who have really read

him—read him with responsive intelligence—know that it
certainly isn't the merely and vaguely inclusive value it might
evoke that answers to the essential intention, for with equal
certainty this last excludes the value the word carries when
Lawrence evokes a person of whom, though he is certainly not
a corpse, it is conveyed to us that his distinctive characteristic is
to be *not* alive. Lawrence, had he commented on George Eliot's
Grandcourt, might have said that of *him*.

In the lucidly expository *Psychoanalysis and the Unconscious* he
necessarily uses 'alive', 'living' and 'lives' in the ordinary variety
of forces inhering in the verb as commonly employed. Yet that
doesn't in the least take from his power to charge 'life' with the
special Laurentian value that gives the word what, for him, is
its supreme use—a use in which it is intimately associated with
'wonder', the 'unknown', 'imagination', 'religious' and 'responsible'. His power to do this is his major-writer's mastery of the
English language: the creativity is one with the thought. He
actually says somewhere: 'Art-speech is the only speech.' And
when, after reading *Psychoanalysis and the Unconscious* and the
Fantasia, we re-read the novels and the tales, we see with a new
realization that the vitality of Lawrence's thought is one with his
extraordinary power of living—the gift of being receptively open
and unafraid in the multifarious human world, and of spontaneously (always with penetrating insight) taking a delicate, truly
delicate, interest in an immense variety of human beings; of
individuals as such, and that is, of life.

His general pronouncements about the novel make plain his
sense that the fictively imaginative achieved art and the expository
modes, springing from the one root, are vitalized by the one sap,
and that there can be no question of a genetic or dynamic priority
to be assigned to either of them. Nevertheless it is plain that he
sees himself primarily as a novelist—as the Laurentian novelist.
In the essay containing the paragraph that deplores the split
between philosophy and the novel, the previous paragraph
runs:

Supposing a bomb were put under the whole scheme of things, what
would we be after? What feelings do we want to carry through into
the next epoch? What feelings will carry us through? What is the
underlying impulse in us that will provide the motive power for a

new state of things, when this democratic-lovey-dovey-darling-take-
me-to-mama state of things is bust?

This certainly describes thought, but hardly what the word
'philosophy' suggests. 'The novel,' he says in the essay that
Phoenix I prints next but one, 'is the highest example of subtle
interrelatedness that man has discovered.' It is by 'subtle interrelatedness' that Lawrence does with current words what dictionary
definition can never do. Take the word 'life'; to the theme it
presents us with, the Laurentian approach is essentially not
philosophical—but how *could* a real approach be that? In the
same essay he says: 'When the man in *Crime and Punishment*
murders the old woman for sixpence, although it is actual enough,
it is never quite real. The balance between the murderer and the
old woman is gone entirely; it is only a mess. It is actuality, but it
is not "life", in the living sense.' In another essay (a much longer
one—'The Reality of Peace') he says: 'For we must all die.
But we need not all live.'

Those familiar with Lawrence's novels and tales will not
assume that in such utterances there is any irresponsibility; the
thought depends upon the indefinables that explain them. Only
a major creative writer can give concrete specificity to such values
and establish them; he does it *in* communicating them: the communicating, or the making communicable, is essential to the
thought. In a Lawrence novel or tale it is done, you can say, by
the subtle interrelatednesses that form the web of imagined and
evoked experience. But it all goes back to words—words used to
form and establish thought; thought which, being neither merely
private nor in the ordinary sense public, belongs, as the words do,
to the Third Realm (the contents or constituents of which can't
be brought into a laboratory, tripped over or even pointed
to).

Eliot's *Four Quartets* forgoes the kinds of human interrelatedness that are entailed by the novel in its aspect of a representative
and intimate human history—a history concretely evoked to be
purely significant in relation to certain inner questionings and
intuitions that profoundly solicit the novelist. Eliot *has* to forgo
any possible afforded advantage—and I think there are many:
he is without the essential powers of a novelist, and such

comments as he makes on novels suggest, in their helplessness or plain fatuity, that he hasn't begun to be intelligently interested. Here we have again the basic contradiction that frustrates the poet's effort of thought. His genius lies in his 'musical' invention, which has some striking local impressiveness. He has to rely, without the resources of a novelist, on his masterful daring with the English language to build up his 'music', which is a music of constructive thought. But still in the late 1930s he seems to have retained something of the incapacity for any but an extraordinarily defective sense of the nature of language that had gone with his Francophilia.

He says in that Introduction of 1924 to 'Le Serpent' which I have referred to:

And at the same time he is a continuator of the experiment, the enquiry, pursued by Mallarmé. As M. Thibaudet rightly says: 'Tout Mallarmé consiste en ceci: une expérience désintéressée sur les confins de la poésie, à une limite où l'air respirable manquerait à d'autres poitrines. Valéry a pris conscience de cette expérience, l'a contrôlée, en a tenté la théorie, a contribué pour sa part à lui donner un commencement d'institution.'

This (endorsed by Eliot) is fatuous in its meaninglessness; la poésie—'sur les confins de la poésie'—is the posited blankly pure 'poetry' of the rebuke that Eliot administers to Blake for not taking over from a professional what of philosophy he needed, and confining his own creative efforts to the poetry. It is not, revealingly not, thought that posits 'poetry' as something that can have 'confines'; and such creative thought as Eliot commits himself to in Four Quartets (the 'music' of which actually entails self-commitment to creative battle) must take place, not on any confines, but on frontiers—the frontiers of language, which major creativity advances. When he had become an unambiguously religious poet he wouldn't, no doubt, have volunteered again the more naïve formulations of his Impersonality. But he didn't withdraw them, and seems (with academic encouragement) to have thought that they do him credit. And The Waste Land (1922) is so decidedly on the way to the frankly religious poetry that such a quotation from F. H. Bradley as still appears on the last page of the notes must be seen as ominous:

THOUGHT, WORDS AND CREATIVITY

My external sensations are no less private to myself than are my thoughts or my feelings. In either case my experience falls within my own circle, a circle closed on the outside; and, with all its elements alike, every sphere is opaque to the others which surround it ... In brief, regarded as an existence which appears in a soul, the whole world is peculiar and private to that soul.

Eliot clearly felt that the distinguished philosopher in whom he had so long ago invested gave the authority of profound thought to the Eliotic attitude towards life and humanity—which persists in *Four Quartets*. The note is to this passage in section V of *The Waste Land*:

> I have heard the key
> Turn in the door once and turn once only
> We think of the key, each in his prison
> Thinking of the key, each confirms a prison
> Only at nightfall, aethereal rumours
> Revive for a moment a broken Coriolanus

But for more than one reason it was ill-advised of Eliot to quote that Bradleian passage as lending impressiveness to a conception (and a valuation) he too cherished of his own personal sense of inner isolation. No creative writer aiming at a major achievement should be able *not* to realize that in using the English language for his purpose he is most essentially and intimately a collaborating member of an immemorial community, the changing language being a product of a continuous collaborative creativity. But Eliot, whose argument in *Four Quartets* starts from a belief in utter human abjectness, cannot help implicitly denying that human creativity exists. Here we have the basic self-contradiction of that poem in which he offers to establish the nature of the supremely Real by means of his own poetic art. It *is* skilled and daring art; and illustrates Eliot's brilliant but limited gift for 'thought, words and creativity': it is the totality and spirit and purpose of the 'musical logic' that the self-contradiction disables.

He owes little or nothing in his major poetry to the French poets of the later 19th century. Accidentally, so to speak, they helped him to escape from the world of Tennyson and Swinburne; but the poet to whom he owed his great debt—though he never said so directly (modesty, let us say)—was the supreme

31

poet of the English language. The Symbolists, to whom, half-a-century ago, he introduced me, were very different from one another, but had most, if not all of them, an acquaintance with English, and I have sometimes thought that, though none of them is Shakespearian, the liberties they took with *la clarté* and *la logique* were inspired by liberties that come, or should come, more naturally to Shakespeare's fellow-countrymen.

Lawrence was neither a Frenchman nor a Francophil, and he was a far greater genius than Eliot. The great novelists of the 19th century were the successors of Shakespeare, and for being a great novelist Lawrence had all the qualifications. How naturally and inevitably he was a novelist is plain from the early non-novel, *Twilight in Italy*, which is about an Italian sojourn with Frieda before that first German war. Chapter III, 'The Theatre', shows how the gifts that made him a great novelist made him also as great a critic as there has ever been. It shows what penetration he had turned on Shakespeare. But what I want to stress at the moment is the ease with which he got on with all kinds of casually encountered people. He got on with them so easily because he was spontaneously interested in them, and in a way that was not only inoffensive but irresistible: they were humanity and life, and *he* was obviously without pretensions or designs. This characteristic was the secret of his dramatic power, which made him so different from all other psychologists. Eliot had no dramatic power and no ease. You can reduce his limitations to those two lacks—which themselves are closely associated. Lawrence the great novelist and critic *is* the great psychologist.

There seems point in closing with the two brief references to E. M. Forster which he made by the way in letters to Martin Secker, his publisher.

Am reading A Passage to India. It's good, but makes one wish a bomb would fall and end it all. Life is more interesting in its undercurrents than in its obvious; and E. M. does see people, people and nothing but people ad nauseam.

This is dated 13 July, 1926. A year later he writes:

St Mawr a bit disappointing. The Bloomsbury highbrows hated it. Glad they did. Don't send any more of my books to E. M. Forster—done with him as with most people. Vogue la galère.

THOUGHT, WORDS AND CREATIVITY

But Lawrence couldn't but go on manifesting the creativity of Laurentian genius till the day of his death in 1930—the historic year when Kingsley Martin became the first editor of the combined *New Statesman and Nation*. The coincidence has a certain felicity; for the journalistic development that culminated in the launch of Martin's career has a crucial bearing on my theme. He was portentously successful; he multiplied again and again the sales of the new *New Statesman*. At a cost, of course—but to him and the supporting élite what I call 'cost' was a triumph of enlightened virtue.

II

'MY MOST IMPORTANT THING SO FAR'

I THINK of myself as an anti-philosopher, which is what a literary critic ought to be—and every intelligent reader of creative literature is a literary critic. At any rate, I know I am not a philosopher. My disclaimer has a positive purpose; one that bears on the conception of literary criticism and of creative literature too. 'Aesthetic' is a word I have little use for; one has to find one's own way of conveying the judgment that *this*, in its livingness, is unmistakably a manifestation of the genuine artist's kind of creativity. I am always, in my dealings with literature, concerned with that order of judgment. But one can't be so concerned without the question of importance entering in. To generalize the question: why does it matter that in university 'English' there should be a genuine and intelligent study of creative writing?

You know how this leads to a statement of the conviction—it seems to me a truism—that the English School should be a liaison-centre, the distinctive function of the university being to restore and maintain the educated public, responsible and influential, that is so disastrously lacking today. I never find myself using the phrase, 'the educated public'—and I know I use it a great deal—without wondering how, if challenged, I should set about explaining what I mean by 'educated'. There would be no point in trying to do it by moderately brief definition; it couldn't be done in any way that answers to the normal sense of 'definition' at all. But the challenge in the very nature of things is profoundly active all the while in my mind and imaginative realization when I discuss Lawrence.

Any intelligent attempt to characterize the distinctive Laurentian genius will bear in a peculiarly direct way on the answer to the challenge. I intimate Lawrence's rare kind of importance— importance for strictly *literary* criticism, properly conceived—

when I say this. Having considered critically his work from a given point of view, I perhaps shall be able, referring back in a suggestion of summary, to give the expected brief kind of answer to the question that preoccupies me: what do I mean by 'an educated public'? But no such brief answer will be an answer. This book is the only kind of real answer I can give.

I will start my critical considering with the novel that, of all Lawrence's, I like least: *The Plumed Serpent*. Lawrence, however, valued it highly. Several years ago, in a limited edition, a collection of his letters to Martin Secker appeared, and someone sent me a copy. I see there that on the 18th of June, 1925, referring to *The Plumed Serpent*, he told Secker: 'It won't be easily popular, but in my opinion it is my most important thing so far.' I haven't read all through the letters in Aldous Huxley's collection since I reviewed it on its first appearance (1932), but, guided by the index, I find that in a letter to Curtis Brown, the literary agent, he wrote of the unpublished book: 'I consider this my most important novel, so far.' The form of the testimony that Catherine Carswell, a close and highly respected friend, supplies in *The Savage Pilgrimage* (page 49) is still more challenging: 'Until he wrote *The Plumed Serpent* he considered *Women in Love* his most important novel.' C. H. Rickword, who reviewed *The Plumed Serpent* in *The Calendar of Modern Letters*, made no such comparative judgment; he merely wrote a decidedly adverse review of *The Plumed Serpent* when it appeared.

Since I shall use that review in my own discussion of Lawrence's novel, I had better say why I think it worth using—and why I shall do my best to get my account of the importance and significance of *The Calendar* generally accepted. That literary organ, the full title of which intimates sufficiently what function it undertook for itself, ran—starting in 1925—for two and a half years, and, for lack of support, ceased publication in mid-1927. It was very intelligent and very lively, and its failure to win the interest and loyalty of a sufficient public to keep it alive has a final kind of significance. The 1920s were the days of Georgian Poetry, the manning of the new English School at Cambridge by second-rate or unlucky Firsts in Classics, Jack Squire's *The London Mercury*, Murry's *The Adelphi*, and Hugh Walpole, Book Society

classic, one of whose novels—he was the son of a bishop (colonial)
—Eliot serialized in *The Criterion*. The failure of *The Calendar*
meant that the educated public, as a public, had ceased to matter—
had in effect disappeared; the 1914 war, which killed so many
young men and prodigiously accelerated the developments, the
inherent processes of our civilization, had so rapidly achieved
that portentous cultural change.

What was final was the proof that there would be no point in
repeating *The Calendar*; a serious critical organ couldn't be run
on commercial lines. That is the kind of thing you might, forty-
five years or so ago, have heard me saying in our drawing-room
on any one of those weekly At Home Fridays out of which
Scrutiny was to issue and from which it was to be recruited until
the second war at last broke on us, and our contributing connexion
was dispersed; for some years the customary source of reinforce-
ment was out of action.

Here, then, you have an essential strand of cultural history—of
literary history—that I myself shall never write. You have,
addressed to a large public of serious readers of whom it is
assumed that their interest in literature is associated with the
diverse other intellectual interests natural to a general cultivation,
the quarterlies and the other weighty reviews of the time of
George Eliot. Then, in the later part of the century, you have the
development represented by *The Savoy* and *The Yellow Book*.
It is the period (with Pater in the background) of Oscar Wilde,
Aestheticism and Willie Yeats. I will—by way of emphasizing
that real literary creativity was affected by the development,
the climatic change—reinforce the suggestion of that last name by
adding that Henry James published in *The Yellow Book*.

No one whose concern is with the relation between creative
writers and the prevailing 'climate', and so with the critical
function as it affects the public—or doesn't affect any public—
will merely associate the 'Nineties (say) with Aestheticism and
The Yellow Book. There was an essential change. One thinks of it
in terms of Northcliffe's exploitation of the opportunities opened
by the historic Education Act that established universal education;
the effect on society of the vulgarization attendant on the influx
of South African gold; Kipling; the writers, English and foreign,
Yeats didn't like—as opposed to those he did; and the ethos,

the sustained drive, leading up to that culminating Boer War which is among my earliest memories. The characteristic of the change most relevant to my preoccupation was one that made, whatever great genius the age might produce, the production of a Dickens so very decidedly impossible. The actual Charles Dickens had died in 1870, the year of the Act. I think of him as our second—and last—Shakespeare.

I won't offer to enlarge on this brief and merely allusive recall of the historical background to *Scrutiny*, but will proceed at once to a specific twentieth-century matter-of-fact that one was conscious of as directly relevant to the enterprise that started in the early 'Thirties. By 'one' I mean 'I'. I had before the 1914 war come on *The English Review* as (for a very short time) it was under the editorship of Ford Madox Ford, or Hueffer. He made it an important fact in the essential history of our kind of concern-and-effort (for such a concern, which can't be merely theoretical, *is* at the same time effort).

The conditions developing in the cultural phase I have just described as making the emergence of a Dickensian genius henceforth impossible necessarily engendered the attitude that was later to find expression in the word 'highbrow'. The distinction of Ford's *English Review* was that its very intelligently active defence and promotion of the finer creativity was adapted to the irreversible new conditions: it accepted as one of them the restriction of concern for the higher cultural values to a small minority, while conceding nothing to the preciousness, fatuity or spirit of Aestheticism. Under Ford it was decidedly a literary review, and he gave proof of his critical perception, and of the courage of it, in his editorial policy.

It was natural for Miriam, of the Eastwood intelligentsia, Lawrence's milieu, to send her lover's poems to Ford, and characteristic of Ford to see that Lawrence was a man to be backed. I myself first read Lawrence in *The English Review*, though I didn't notice that it was Lawrence I was reading; Lawrence wasn't then a known name. After the war, starting to sample something in a book, *The Prussian Officer*, I had pulled down from the First Class shelves of the Union Library at Cambridge, I had an uncanny sense that it was familiar, and, collecting myself, suddenly realized that it was a tale I had read in *The English*

Review half-a-dozen years earlier—in 1912, it must have been. For the number I had was a back-number, an advertisement copy I had sent for. I subscribed.

But Ford, the brilliant editor (that is his claim to be remembered) wasn't to last much longer; he probably knew already he was being sacked. He must have known, at any rate, that he wasn't satisfactory to the proprietors. Well before the outbreak of the war he was replaced by Austin Harrison, son of Frederic Harrison, George Eliot's positivist friend—who was still alive and writing letters to *The Times* when I got back to Cambridge. With Austin Harrison as editor, *The English Review* ceased to be a great literary organ—or, if I can trust my memory, a literary organ at all. He was sure that the war was coming, and that the important thing was to warn the country against the German menace—a conviction that editorial policy enforced. I, a green boy (today I should have had the vote) didn't read him, or the intellectuals he printed.

From Ford's *English Review* to *The Calendar of Modern Letters* is a leap of a dozen years. By 1925, the year that saw the start of *The Calendar*, the consequences of that fatal war for the critical function and for the critically conscious minority public, mutually dependent as they inevitably were, could no longer fail to justify the desperate apprehensions of the concerned and informed. But it was still possible to suppose that the apprehensions were more widely felt—more often with coercive strength—than they proved to be. After all, the decade was Bloomsbury's, whose self-flattering illusions were fortified with snob-social superiority and cohesion, and endorsed by the kind of recognition attendant on these.

The group that launched *The Calendar* had a cohesion that was *ad hoc*—one, that is, of a very different kind. How the group had formed itself I don't know; I met, and that briefly, only one of the half-dozen: Douglas Garman. He had, after the Armistice, come up to Cambridge, and he shared the editing with Edgell Rickword, who, I am pretty sure, hadn't. Both these, at any rate, were survivors of the war. I've had to deduce this about Rickword, but know I'm right because I remember the line:

> I saw him kill and kill again a well-killed Boche

from a poem of his called 'The Happy Warrior'. The poem, I
think, was one of those collected in his *Invocations to Angels*, a
book that I lost long ago, though I recall not only the title, but
the opening lines of the title-poem:

> Angels, bequeath your tongues of flame
> To those who need them more than you.

I bring out such casually prompted recollections because they
help to suggest the edged and toughened quality, the bite clearly
favoured by the editors in the criticism they wished to see as
making *The Calendar*'s performance of the function distinctive.
The actual distinctiveness was so much not superficial that I
found myself guessing at some strong and very effective personal
influence as accounting for it—influence educational in a way
capable of initiating the shared acceptance of *The Calendar* as a
desperately needed enterprise, one that must be carried on with
full vigour and conviction if it was to have any chance of success.

My efforts to get *Towards Standards of Criticism* reissued as a
paperback have been unsuccessful. That book, as students who
have discussed Valéry's 'Le Cimetière Marin' with me know,
was the selection from the critical work of *The Calendar* I per-
suaded the firm of Wishart to bring out in 1933. It has been
unobtainable since before the last war, but my introduction to it
is included in *Anna Karenina and Other Essays*.

You will have gathered from my brief account of *The Calendar*,
and from my hints at the place I would assign to it in cultural
history, that I regard with great respect the team of critics who
performed the critical function in its pages. I *say* that now because
in the discussion, to which I at length turn, of Lawrence's *The
Plumed Serpent* I shall quote passages from C. H. Rickword's
review of that novel in order to disagree with them. The review
is decidedly adverse, but my disagreement doesn't mean that I
share Lawrence's own valuation of *The Plumed Serpent*. I don't.
In fact, the explaining how he could judge it the most important
thing he had so far done, and, presumably, a better novel than
Women in Love—in any case, a more important one—faces me
with what might very well look like something of a problem.
The problem, however, is a challenge that repays the taking-up,
because the thinking we enter on in considering it fosters a

completer understanding of Lawrence's genius and thought. As for the misconceptions of the reviewer, they suggest how difficult that thought was to adjust oneself to, when the work was first published. A critic who succeeded in getting anything like an intelligently responsive public for the Laurentian communication would have started a portentous change in the civilized consciousness.

I point here, in these last reflections, to the how and the why of my finding C. H. R., who is so far from being that critic, a useful, if unintending and unconscious, collaborator in my attempt to explain Lawrence's high estimate of a novel I find, and have always found, unsatisfactory. That the review is going to be hostile in a way in which I can't concur the opening paragraph makes plain:

> Mr Lawrence, in this book, is ostensibly concerned to reveal a sense of the significance of life so profound and universal that only such comprehensive symbols of the divine in man as Gods are adequate to express it. His theme, also ostensibly, is of a nature so ineffable as to be expressible only in art.

The ironic intention is unmistakable, and the assumptions implicit in the irony are, I think, more fundamentally unacceptable than anything in *The Plumed Serpent*. They are apparent all through C. H. R.'s review, beginning to become explicit in the first sentence of the next paragraph:

> Mr Lawrence's metaphysics, as such, need not detain us; that they are a sentimental vulgarization of the ordinary dualism of subject and object, togged up in the tawdry finery of emotive (often erotic) symbolism, it would be easy to show by a page or two of quotation.

C. H. R., I conjecture, would, if called on to justify his 'easy to show', have filled up his page or two with quoted passages the separation of which, whether brief or lengthy, from their context would have made his criticism less challengeable. But the basic fallacy of this quotation from his review challenges us flatly in its first three words: 'Mr Lawrence's metaphysics.' As I tried to make plain in my opening chapter, his approach to his theme, and his mode of developing his thought, are nowhere a philosopher's, and his aphorism, 'Art-speech is the only speech', bears not only on those imaginative creations of his that are in the full sense creative works, but on his discursive writings too; it is a conclusion (with which I agree, and which I am undertaking to enforce) of the most important kind about the nature of thought.

In any case, there could be no more false and misleading account of the Laurentian modes of thought that C. H. R. calls 'metaphysics' than that 'they are a sentimental vulgarization of the ordinary dualism of subject and object, togged up in the tawdry finery of emotive . . . symbolism'. Actually, C. H. R. is revealing his own disability here, his impotence to escape from 'the ordinary dualism of subject and object'; he is denying Lawrence's originality, which he dismisses as 'togging-up'. 'Hence', he says, with the naïve confidence that attends on his sophistication, 'there is a continuous falsification of reality': C. H. R. implies that *he* knows what reality is—that he has the criteria in his possession. 'The absence of detachment', we read, 'destroys any pretensions to objectivity'. The criteria of objectivity invoked here are essentially those assumed as unquestionable by Andreski in *Social Sciences and Sorcery*.[1]

I mustn't be supposed to be accusing C. H. R. of blank philistinism. He has for some of his none-the-less questionable judgments critical reasons that have their beginning in the reports of sensibility. But the reports of sensibility, not to speak of sensibility itself, may be affected by habits of assumption; and that unquestioned and unexamined routine ideas about objectivity and reality have determined his criticism in ways inimical to valid thought is plain. This—he has just quoted a paragraph—seems to me an instance:

Here, the insistence on the subjective epithets, the hypnotic drumming on the note of death and its harmonics betray the unauthenticity of the response. Contact with the things observed is not immediate, but dissipated and confused by the echoing, emotive overtones. The necessity for constant interpretation of this sort suggests that the experience to be conveyed had not its roots in actuality . . .

I find this certainly confused, and perverse too. What, for example, is implied by 'contact with things', and what is 'actuality'? The critic seems to be concerned to make his meaning

[1] See page 25 ff. of *The Living Principle: 'English' as a Discipline of Thought.*

plain by giving us, as his positive desideratum, 'authenticity'. Our unfavourable conclusions are confirmed by the next sentence, in which he softens his severity by conceding that the novelist (whose work *The Calendar* has published) *can* do better:

> How unnecessary this charlatanism really is can be seen in the isolated passages in which Mr Lawrence confines himself to the setting down of events for their own sake.

Whether or not it is thought possible to 'set down events for their own sake', it is certain that no creative writer could ever do it. C. H. R. should have pondered what is said in the Prologue to *The Calendar* (included in *Towards Standards*, in which the sentences I quote are on page 28): 'The artist, who can differ only in degree and in function from the rest of men, by revealing differences, creates realities.' The crucial phrase here is 'creates realities': the specificities that the great creative writer evokes are always contributory to the creation of some comprehensive reality, some world, that his deep, imaginatively engaged, spontaneity inspires him to create. 'It is through him,' the Prologue goes on, 'that we can perfect our individuality, our own shape, which under the crude strokes of actual experience'—as opposed, that is, to imaginatively created-and-evoked experience—'might remain only roughly chipped out on the surface of that rock of ages, the folk-mind.'

This is a pregnant, if in mode of expression, unLaurentian passage prompting discussion and development which would be out of place now. I will confine myself to considering the particular charge brought against Lawrence as C. H. R. brings it and insists on it in the passage I have quoted of the review: 'Contact with the things observed is not immediate, but dissipated and confused by the echoing, emotive overtones.'

He might have included among the 'isolated passages' that he exempts from the charge of charlatanism the vivid and disturbing opening chapter, 'The Beginnings of a Bull-fight'—except that it is not what 'isolated passage' suggests, but a chapter, and the opening one. It is very plain there that the effect of 'objectivity'—of being put in immediate touch with reality itself—*depends* on the 'echoing, emotive overtones'. The vividness is inseparable from the disgust, the horror, the recoil which the 'things observed' evoke. It would be ridiculous to contend that the events are 'set down for their own sake'; an attempt to justify this phrase would find itself explaining that the vivid 'objectivity' of the facts was a matter of their high emotive 'value', which the novelist had rendered in his prose. A consonant judgment is compelled by that *nouvelle* of Lawrence's, 'The Princess', which the editors printed in instalments in the first three numbers of *The Calendar*, giving it the first place in the opening number.

There is immense diversity of mode among things that are with equal unmistakableness Lawrence. I am not charging C. H. R. with stupid philistinism when I suggest that he would most probably have denied that there was any inconsistency here: his own charge against Lawrence as represented by the passage he quotes from *The Plumed Serpent* is offered as a diagnosis of charlatanism, of insincerity—of a *parti-pris* to inject 'significance'. There is nothing as challengingly overt in its insistent and emphatic intensity in 'The Princess'. What I am concerned to bring out is the resistance on the part of something even in the critical élite of *The Calendar*, something that I will call 'commonsense' (for the new 'commonsense' that Lawrence calls for is very difficult to acquire)—resistance in the way of complete and consistent response to the profound originality of the Laurentian genius. I need quotations in order to enforce my point, which, obvious as it is, is so important as to demand full critical recognition. I will take them from 'The Captain's Doll', one of the supreme products of the genius, and notable for its supple infallibility in a shifting diversity of tone and mode.

It is the last and conclusive phase of the relations between Captain Hepburn and the Countess Hannele, and they are climbing up a valley of the Tyrol towards the glacier which they want to see:

So the two climbed slowly up the steep ledge of a road. The valley was just a mountain cleft, cleft sheer in the hard, living rock, with black trees like hair flourishing in this secret, naked place of the earth. At the bottom of the open wedge forever roared the rampant, insatiable water. The sky from above was like a sharp wedge forcing its way into the earth's cleavage, and that eternal ferocious water was like the steel edge of the wedge, the terrible tip biting into the rock's intensity. Who could have thought that the soft sky of light and the soft foam of water could thrust and penetrate into the dark, strong earth? But so it was.

Would C. H. R. have judged this to be an instance of Lawrence's charlatanism? It is charged heavily with emotive overtones. Where epithets are concerned, who can defend 'rampant', 'insatiable', and 'eternal ferocious' applied to descending water, precipitated down by the force of gravity, or the 'living' of the cliché 'living rock' made to prompt the suggestion of an earth that is a body with 'secret places'? The emotiveness is continued to much the same effect. It is a sustained insistence, having begun earlier. A page before we have (they are as yet in a car):

> To the right was the strong, furious, lion-like river, tawny-coloured here, and the slope up beyond. But the road for the moment was swinging fairly level through the stunned water-meadows of the savage valley.

I don't as a matter-of-fact think that any *Calendar* critic would have stigmatized the prose of this as contemptible charlatanism. C. H. R. would have recognized that its emotiveness was both appropriate and necessary, the 'events' to be 'set down' forming the experience of a Hepburn and a Hannele toiling up an Alpine valley towards a glacier at its head. But such recognition would surrender everything in the critical position out of which he wrote his review. A novelist deals with life as it is lived, and the living of life is always related to a given environment and given events. There is a special appropriateness in the last phase of the delicate and difficult emotional relations between Hepburn and Hannele being identified, as it were, with the changing ardours of the climb, and the appropriateness is not merely a matter of what we are told on the same page as that from which I took my longer quotation:

> He and Hannele also were not in good company together. There was a sort of silent hostility between them.

I won't spend time examining the passage C. H. R. quotes from *The Plumed Serpent* as an example of Lawrence's charlatanism, and pointing out why it doesn't deserve the adverse judgment— so far as I can see, it doesn't deserve to be judged adversely at all.

There are many ways of offending creatively against the sub-jective-objective dualism taken for granted in that *Calendar* review. In fact, it may be said that every genuine creative writer's work is the discovery of a new way. Life is unamenable to mathe-matical or quantificative finality of treatment, and every creative writer is a servant of life. The dualism of subject and object, fact and value—it faces us, unprofitably, with all the problems of epistemology—is hostile to life. C. H. R. is guilty of a profound and unconscious inconsistency in his commonsense confidence of adhesion to it; for we can't doubt that he approved of *The Calendar's* printing, and paying for, that *nouvelle* of Lawrence's, 'The Princess'. When the 'higher commonsense' of a civilization is blank to such an inconsistency, being essentially characterized by it, life is debilitated and imperilled, and only a genius can initiate the liberating transformation needed to restore the life-flow from the deep source. There was certainly distinguished intelligence at the formative centre of the *Calendar* connexion, but no genius.

The genius was Lawrence, but in the half-century since his death the transformation hasn't begun to be achieved: this is the age in which general pro-democratic enlightenment has destroyed the small public on which any effective appeal to serious criteria must depend.

In 1930, the year in which Lawrence died, the computer was not there for him to have heard of it, but in a sense he foresaw it. For his intelligence told him that 'objectivity' as C. H. R. con-ceived it was a deadly fallacy, and that science, which in the course of the recent centuries had invested the assumptions behind 'objectivity' with the authority of clear commonsense, was advancing to new conquests over life at an acceleration. He didn't himself propose any account of the origin of life, but treated all speculation as to how inanimate nature could have generated life with dismissive disrespect. For he was profoundly anti-Cartesian, believing not only that life had always been there, but that the separated pure inanimate nature of natural science was a falsifying abstraction. His 'nothing is important but life' carried with it, not only the knowledge that human ingenuity can make incredibly ingenious machines, but the conviction that the need for life to be rooted in the cosmos was not one-sided.

Thus on page 118 of *Fantasia of the Unconscious* in my edition we read:

From the objective circuits and from the subjective circuits which establish and fulfil themselves at the first four centres of consciousness we derive our first being, our child-being, and also our first mind, our child-mind. By the objective circuits we mean those circuits which are established between the self and some eternal object: mother, father, sister, cat, dog, bird, or even tree or plant, or even further still, some particular place, some inanimate object, a knife or a chair or a cap or a doll or a wooden horse. For we must insist that every object which really enters effectively into our lives does so by direct connection.

If I love my mother, it is because there is established between me and her a direct, powerful circuit of vital magnetism, call it what you will, but a direct flow of dynamic *vital* interchange and intercourse. I will not call this vital flow a *force*, because it depends on the incomprehensible initiative and control of the indivual soul or self. Force is that which is directed only from some universal will or law. Life is *always* individual, and therefore never controlled by one law, one God. And therefore, since the living really sway the universe, even if unknowingly; therefore there is no one universal law, even for the physical forces. Because we insist that even the sun depends for its heart-beat, its respiration, its pivotal motion, on the beating hearts of men and beasts, on the dynamic soul in individual creatures. It is from the aggregate heart-beat of living individuals, of we know not how many or what sort of worlds, that the sun rests stable.

Which may be dismissed as metaphysics, although it is quite as valid or even as demonstrable as Newton's Law of Gravitation, which law still remains a law, even if not quite as absolute as heretofore.

So robustly confident is what I have called the 'commonsense' of the established science-dominated age of human history that some readers, if not most, may shake their heads over the concluding Laurentian assurance. In order that they should not do so with too easy a certitude that *this* may be automatically dismissed as complete and palpable nonsense, I will relate an episode out of my recent experience.

I received a letter from someone I didn't know, but he was by training a scientist, asking me whether I could tell him where it was that Lawrence disputed the scientific correctness of asserting that 'water is H_2O'. He needed the specific reference so that he might give due force to his use of the place in Lawrence as a

'MY MOST IMPORTANT THING SO FAR'

locus classicus, a corrective and salutary formulation and commentary. I, like the inquirer, had read the passage, and had not forgotten it; but I am not the infallible guide to things in Lawrence's immense *oeuvre* that I am sometimes taken to be, and couldn't find it. I wrote to the inquirer to say so. Coming back from the pillar-box I had a hunch what context it belonged to and where it must be. The hunch was quickly confirmed, and my correspondent got a brief second scrawl simultaneously with the first.

The passage comes in 'Introduction to These Paintings', which Mr J. V. Davies has included in the paperback to accompany the long *Study of Thomas Hardy.* These are Lawrence's comments on the assertion that 'water is H_2O' in their immediate context, which bears so pregnantly on my preoccupation and my whole argument—I begin at the bottom of page 151 of the paperback:

But Veronese and Tintoretto are real painters; they are not mere *virtuosi,* as some of the later men are.

The point is very important. Any creative act occupies the whole consciousness of a man. This is true of the great discoveries of science as well as of art. The truly great discoveries of science and real works of art are made by the whole consciousness of man working together in unison and oneness: instinct, intuition, mind, intellect all fused into one complete consciousness, and grasping what we may call a complete truth, or a complete vision, a complete revelation in sound. A discovery, artistic or otherwise, may be more or less intuitional, more or less mental; but intuition will have entered into it and mind will have entered too. The whole consciousness is concerned in every case. And a painting requires the activity of the whole imagination, for it is made of imagery, and the imagination is that form of the complete consciousness in which predominates the intuitive awareness of forms, images, the *physical* awareness.

And the same applies to the genuine appreciation of a work of art, or the *grasp* of a scientific law, as to the production of the same. The whole consciousness is occupied, not merely the mind alone, or merely the body. The mind and spirit alone can never really grasp a work of art, though they may, in a masturbating fashion, provoke the body into an ecstasized response. The ecstasy will die out into ash and more ash. And the reason we have so many trivial scientists promulgating fantastic 'facts' is that so many modern scientists likewise work with the mind alone, and *force* the intuitions and instincts into a prostituted acquiescence. The very statement that water *is* H_2O is a mental *tour de force.* With our bodies we know that water is *not* H_2O, our intuitions

47

and instincts both know it is not so. But they are bullied by the impudent mind. Whereas if we said that water, under certain circumstances, produces two volumes of hydrogen and one of oxygen, then the intuitions and instincts would agree entirely. But that water *is composed* of two volumes of hydrogen to one of oxygen we cannot physically believe. It needs something else. Something is missing. Of course, alert science does not ask us to believe the commonplace assertion of: *water* is H_2O, but school children have to believe it.

After two further paragraphs, Lawrence writes: 'Which brings me back to Cézanne, and why he couldn't draw, and why he couldn't paint baroque masterpieces.' I, without such cogently direct and obvious sequentiality, come back, after my long quotation, to *The Plumed Serpent*, and why I judge it to be an unsatisfactory novel, a question which is prior to the hardly separable one: why Lawrence should have judged it to be the most important thing he had yet done. Prior, because the point of the second question is that one can't agree with Lawrence's judgment. I substituted 'one' for 'I' in this last sentence because I think that few admirers of Lawrence *have* agreed with him about *The Plumed Serpent*.

I return to the first person because a real judgment is necessarily personal, though it aims to be more than merely that. I've made it fairly plain that my reasons for not thinking the novel a highly successful one are not C. H. R.'s. But for his review it wouldn't have occurred to me that anyone could accuse Lawrence of charlatanism. I won't, however, pretend that when I first read the review in *The Calendar* I was moved to indignant protest, or even inclined to argue against it. I hadn't in the middle 1920s had enough literary experience to be even incipiently intelligent about him. But this way of putting it doesn't suggest the nature of the challenge he presented: I most certainly wasn't capable in those days of a critical appreciation of his importance. But how could anyone in the 1920s have been, except a genius? Who was there in literary criticism that impressed one as worth intensive pondering but Eliot—whose impressiveness turned out to be so largely illusion? In any case, his thought at its best, even if there had been more of it, could hardly help one to adjust oneself to Lawrence's. Only Lawrence's was qualified to do that, and *he* demanded that one should transcend—transcend so impossibly—

the commonsense, the whole cultural ethos, in which one had been brought up, and in terms of which one did one's thinking. That was the dilemma—the dilemma that one was not capable of stating. And this account covers, inevitably, C. H. R.'s case too, though he had the advantage of sharing in the special play of cultivated intelligence behind *The Calendar*.

That this advantage was not pure advantage the opening paragraph of his review evidences: 'Mr Lawrence, in this book, is ostensibly concerned etc. ... His theme, also ostensibly, is of a nature so ineffable etc. . . .' The obvious ironical intention comes out in the repeated 'ostensibly'. Plainly, the convictions, the basic intuitive certitudes, that inform Lawrence's thought and art were not such as to recommend themselves to C. H. R., who can be regarded as representing the stance and tone characteristic of the permanent central group in which the drive behind *The Calendar* was focused. I use the words 'stance' and 'tone' because, though the key members of the centre were undoubtedly very intelligent, you can't attribute to them any common ground of worked out thought.

The 'stance' and 'tone' were those of militant conviction, but the conviction, honestly enough (life has to be lived, and one learns, if at all, in the living), was the 'ostensibly' firm overlay to basic, largely contradictory, non-thought. Veterans they were still young; the monstrous war lay in the background, and disillusioning memory, in which Horatio Bottomley had his part, was potent in them—and even the 1920s was not an encouraging decade to be alive in. They had believed enough in creative effort to commit themselves to *The Calendar*; but they sheered off from idealisms and optimisms. The contradictions inherent in the underlying vague uncertainty about fundamentals are apparent in the contrasting two reviews of I. A. Richards that *The Calendar* did. That of *The Principles* was written by Edgell Rickword; he liked the book (Garman, talking to me, said 'we'— so it was discussed). The review is a respectful one, making some basic discriminations by the way to the disadvantage of the weak or questionable in what is a very mixed book, but emphasizing that which Rickword found he could respond to favourably. It plays down the clear and strong bent towards pseudo-science and neo-Benthamism. Later, *Science and Poetry* was reviewed—

again, I gathered from the reviewer, after discussion—by Douglas Garman. In that little book there was nothing to disguise or blur what the author really stood for, and could be relied on to continue standing for, in the cultural ethos of our then cock-a-hoop civilization. 'It is noticeable at once that Mr Richards is more convinced of the value of Science than that of Poetry, for in this short book he devotes much space and many clichés to the discussion of the latter, confidently leaving the former to speak for itself.' This is the first sentence of Garman's appropriately short review, which is a frankly contemptuous dismissal.

Nevertheless, the ironical first paragraph of C. H. R.'s review of *The Plumed Serpent* is significant: the *Calendar* attitude, a dissatisfied one, towards Western civilization was not conscious enough about fundamentals to be truly and consistently radical. That is betrayed by the inconsistency itself; the contradiction (for instance) between serializing 'The Princess' in the first three numbers and guying the essential Laurentian convictions in the opening paragraph of C. H. R.'s review. The concluding sentence of that review runs: 'Of the earnestness of Mr Lawrence's intentions and the vigour, even violence, of his impulse (that at times compels him to break into verse) there can be no question; the seriousness and integrity of either are, however, another matter.'

When I met Garman, *The Calendar* belonged to the past, having ceased publication because it had become plain that it would never cease to depend on a subsidy. No doubt that collapse of enterprise and hope had confirmed the un-Laurentian 'stance' and 'tone'; I remember Garman's saying that he had nothing to look forward to but a miserable middle-age. He was intelligent, handsome and a gentleman—obviously (to recall the old pre-blood-bath criteria for commissions) 'officer-material'. Whether he had become, or was becoming, a Marxist or fellow-traveller I can't say, but I thought I detected some such development in his attitude. I deduced from things he said that Wishart's relations with *The Calendar* hadn't been merely commercial, or commercial at all. Wishart was the publisher of *The Calendar*, and, subsequent to the correspondence involved in my doing (for love) the work for *Towards Standards*, Wishart was replaced by Lawrence and Wishart, which was avowedly a Marxist publishing-house.

It is time I gave my own reasons for a decidedly adverse judgment on the work that Lawrence pronounced the most important
thing he had yet done, though *Women in Love* had come before.
I have always been ready to say, till now, that *The Plumed Serpent*
is the longest of all Lawrence's novels. I was intending to say it
again, when it occured to me, since that one of Lawrence's
novels, with several others, lay handy on my desk, to verify the
fact before writing. Among the others was *Women in Love*, and
my first comparison was with that: I found that the earlier novel
was at least 15,000 words longer than *The Plumed Serpent*. I was
surprised, though not disconcerted for I took the discovery as
confirming an essentially critical judgment, one I had implicitly
passed on *The Plumed Serpent* every time I read it—and I have
read it through three times recently in not many more weeks.

Those re-readings have made it clear to me that the critical
judgment compelled is a major one—for my critical reactions
have, of course, at no time been merely implicit, and judgment,
largely tentative at first, has achieved confirmation, reinforce-
ment and greater fullness. The illusion as to length was due to my
finding the book slow-going, as I have always done. But the
significance of that repeated experience requires thought and
delicate statement.

The theme of *The Plumed Serpent* as announced in that title is
the imagined revival and re-establishment of the old Mexican
religion. The unfairness—the palpable animus—of C. H. R.'s
Calendar review begins, as I said, with the first sentence: 'Mr
Lawrence, in this book, is ostensibly concerned to reveal a sense
of the significance of life so profound and universal that only such
comprehensive symbols of the divine in man as Gods are adequate
to express it.' But there is nothing ecstatic, intoxicated, wallowing
or not vitally compelled about Lawrence's preoccupation with
religion in *The Plumed Serpent*. The preoccupation remains
essentially Laurentian—that of the man who said: 'Thank God,
I am not free any more than a rooted tree is free'; and this concern for life as opposed to automatism has the full delicate, firm
and marvellously informed thought-context as we have it in
Psychoanalysis and the Unconscious.

How central the tree-image is to Laurentian thought comes out,
in *The Plumed Serpent*, in what Don Ramón says to Kate, who

remains haunted and oppressed by the nighmare sinisterness of Mexico:

'They pull you down! Mexico pulls you down, the people pull you down like a great weight! But it may be they pull you down as the earth's pull of gravitation does, that you can balance on it. Maybe they draw you down as the earth draws down the roots of a tree, so that it may be clinched deep in soil. Men are still part of the Tree of Life, and its roots go down to the centre of the earth. Loose leaves, aeroplanes, blow away on the wind, in what they call freedom. But the Tree of Life has fixed, deep, gripping roots.

It may be that you need to be drawn down, down, till you send roots into the deep places again. Then you can send up the sap and the leaves back to the sky, later.

And to me the men in Mexico are like trees, forests that the white men felled in their coming. But the roots of the trees are deep and alive and forever sending up new shoots.

And each new shoot that comes up overthrows a Spanish church or an American factory.

. . . The roots and the life are there. What also it needs is the word, for the forest to begin to rise again. And some man among men must speak the word'.

The strange doom-like sound of the man's words! But in spite of the sense of doom on her heart, she would not go away yet. She would stay longer in Mexico.

Ramón himself is the man who 'speaks the word'. As for 'God', the word which C. H. R. puts in the plural by way of expressing contempt—at the cost of falsifying the communication made by the book he is reviewing—the significance of that word is brought out in this context of talk with Kate on the same occasion:

'I?' he laughed. 'I spent a long time trying to pretend, I thought I could have my own way. Till I realized that having my own way meant only running about smelling all the things in the street, like a dog that will pick up something. Of myself I have no way. No man has any way in himself. Every man who goes along a way is led by one of three things: by an appetite—and I class ambition among appetites; or by an idea; or by an inspiration.'

'I used to think my husband was inspired about Ireland,' Kate said doubtfully.

'And now?'

'Yes! Perhaps he put his wine into old bottles that wouldn't hold it.

No!—Liberty is an old rotten wine-skin. It won't hold one's wine of inspiration or passion any more,' she said.

'And Mexico!' he said. 'Mexico is another Ireland. Ah no, no man can be his own master. If I must serve, I will not serve an idea, which cracks and leaks like an old wine-skin. ... Free Mexico is a bully, and the old, colonial ecclesiastical Mexico was another sort of bully. When a man has nothing but his *will* to assert—even his good-will—it is always bullying. Bolshevism is one kind of bullying, capitalism another: and liberty is a change of chains.'

'Then what's to be done?' said Kate. 'Just nothing?'

* * *

'One is driven, at last, back to the far distance, to look for God,' said Ramón uneasily.

'I rather hate this search-for-God business, and religiosity,' said Kate.

'I know!' he said, with a laugh. 'I've suffered from would-be-cock-sure religion myself.'

'And you can't *really* find God!' she said. 'It's a sort of sentimentalism, and creeping back into old, hollow shells.'

'No!' he said slowly. 'I can't *find God*, in the old sense. I know it's a sentimentalism if I pretend to. But I am nauseated with humanity and the human will: even with my own will. I have realized that *my own will*, no matter how intelligent I am, is only a nuisance on the face of the earth, once I start exerting it. And other people's *wills* are even worse.'

'Oh! isn't human life horrible!' she cried. 'Every human being exerting his will all the time—over other people, and righteous.'

Ramón made a face of repulsion.

'To me,' he said, 'That is just the weariness of life. ... My soul is nauseated, and there is nothing but death ahead, unless I can find something else.'

There you have the theme, the drive in Eliot's religious poetry—the drive to the quest that, in 'Little Gidding', ended in happy surrender that one part of him took for safe arrival, at last, in harbour: 'Little Gidding', the poet's last poem—to be followed by *The Cocktail Party*!

Ramón goes on:

'My own will, merely as my own will, is even more distasteful to me than other people's wills. From being the God in my own machine, I must either abdicate, or die of disgust—self-disgust at that.' ...

53

'And then?', she asked, looking at him with a certain malevolent challenge.

He looked back at her slowly, with an ironical light in his eyes.

'Then!' he repeated. 'Then!—I ask, what else is there in the world, besides human will, human appetite? because ideals and ideas are only instruments of human will and appetite.'

'Not entirely,' said Kate. 'They may be disinterested.'

'May they? If the appetite isn't interested, the will is.'

'Why not?' she mocked. 'We can't be mere detached blocks.'

'It nauseates me—I look for something else.'

'And what do you find?'

'My own manhood!'

'What does that mean?' she cried, jeering.

'If you looked, and found your own womanhood, you would know.'

'But I *have* my own womanhood!' she cried.

'And then—when you find your own manhood—your womanhood,' he went on, smiling faintly at her—'then you know it is not your own, to do as you like with. You don't have it of your own will. It comes from—from the middle—from the God. And the God gives me my manhood, then leaves me to it. I have nothing but my manhood. The God gives it me, and leaves me to do further.'

This constatation as it is put in *Psychoanalysis and the Unconscious* is part of a discursive exposition of the organic complexity of life in the individual being—life as it develops into full 'createdness'. This—a comparatively rare consummation—has (this is the implicit datum) been achieved in Ramón, and with it the responsibility he recognizes as his. He has already 'spoken the word'; the revival of the old Mexican religion has already begun.

The Gods (Quetzalcoatl and Huitzilopochtli) whose resurrection Ramón prompts, initiates and fosters, are not to be crudely identified in C. H. R.'s way with 'the God'—'at the middle'—who gives Ramón his manhood, and then leaves him to it. Nevertheless, they are the necessary means, his responsibility tells him, of putting the Mexican masses in touch with the 'beyond' from which his own manhood, his recognized but unwilled responsibility, comes to him. Here we have the difficulties and the delicacies that make the essential difference between *The Plumed Serpent* and Lawrence's other novels. Had C. H. R. been in a position to write the review of *The Plumed Serpent* that no

one *could* have written in the 1920s, he would not have charged
Lawrence with charlatanism or failure of integrity, but have
discussed the ways in which the blame—if there was to *be* blame—
for the inferiority of the book as a novel must rest on Mexico.

Lawrence's devoted concern for the life-theme, together with
the manifest intensity of his interest in Mexico, an intimately
related pre-occupation, though the two were not to be identified,
faced him—and faces us—with an exquisitely delicate problem.
He must inevitably lie under the suspicion of having yielded, at
least a little, to temptation—the temptation to identify them; we
have naturally, in the nature of the case, a strong sense of the
temptation.

How, we ask, came Lawrence to write this—it comes from a
long allocution (it is certainly not conversational, or in any
obvious sense dramatic) addressed by Ramón to his intimate
associate and friend, Cipriano?—

'Only from the flowers there is commingling. And the flowers of
every race are the natural aristocrats of that race. . . . Only the Natural
Aristocrats can rise above their nation; and even they do not rise
beyond their race. Only the Natural Aristocrats of the World can be
international, cosmopolitan, or cosmic. It has always been so. The
people are no more capable of it than the leaves of the mango tree are
capable of attaching their leaves to the pine.—So if I want Mexicans
to learn the name of Quetzalcoatl, it is because I want them to speak
with the tongues of their own blood. I wish the Teutonic world
would once more think in terms of Thor or Wotan, and the tree
Ygdrasil. And I wish the Druidic world would see, honestly, that in
the mistletoe is their mystery, and that they themselves are the Tuatha
De Danaan, alive, but submerged. And a new Hermes would come
back to the Mediterranean, and a new Ashtaroth to Tunis; and Mithras
again to Persia, and Brahma unbroken to India, and the oldest of
dragons to China. . . . Ah, the earth has valleys of the soul that are not
cities of commerce and industry. And the mystery is one mystery, but
men must see it differently.'

Of course, this is attributed to Ramón, the Aristocrat of virtually pure Spanish blood who nevertheless is a Mexican. But I
find no hint that Lawrence himself thinks of it as anything but
an emphasis, and a sound one, on the relevance of the imagined
Mexican possibility to the problem as it torments the Birkins.

There *is*, of course, a relevance; but what Ramón (and Lawrence through him) is unwittingly emphasizing is the immense difference that makes his Mexican anti-Crusade seem utterly irrelevant to *Women in Love*: the great bulk of the Mexican population consists of ignorant peasant Indians, deep in whom, whether tradition may be said to remember it or not, resides the conquest with its consequences, among which is resentment at the gringo-domination.

Lawrence, with his 'my most important thing so far', is insisting on the essential relevance. And he is in a way justified in doing this. In his study of an actual country which he has observed from close up with the astonishing insight of genius, a country so utterly unlike any that Europe can suggest, he is testing and confirming his essential thought, and, for the reader, extending the contextual field.

And this is the point at which to refer to *Mornings in Mexico*; to—in especial—the marvellous evocations there of 'the Dance of the Sprouting Corn' and 'the Hopi Snake Dance'. These, in their marvellousness, are truly important—with an importance that proves itself in the compelling art in which the Indian, the utterly non-Western, 'commonsense' is made an indisputable reality for us. The astonishing creativity is perception, the imagination that informs it is unmistakably intuitive apprehension, insight real and not imaginary. How profoundly Lawrence was impressed by what intuition brought home to him is evidenced by one of his most impressive tales: 'The Woman Who Rode Away'. The imagination that created this was not arbitrary; it was devoted, with all its powers, to realizing a truth. And the truth *is* crucially important; it enforces Lawrence's contention that what the West desperately needs is a new kind of 'commonsense'. It doesn't, of course, follow that the answer to the West's malaise would, or could, be the Mexican Indian solution—or, rather, on the lines of what Ramón prescribed for his Mexico. But Mexico's clear confirmation of Lawrence's anti-Benthamite intuition would in itself explain his judgment about *The Plumed Serpent*.

I have no doubt, too, that a sense of the very urgency that is an aspect of the odds against such an undertaking as Ramón's had its part in Lawrence's sense of the 'thing's' relative importance. The following comes in *Mornings in Mexico* a couple of paragraphs from the end of section 8, which contains those marvellous evocations of the ritual dances:

The American aborigines are radically, innately religious. The fabric of their life is religion. But their religion is animistic, their sources are dark and impersonal, and their conflict with their 'gods' is slow, and unceasing.

This is true of the settled pueblo Indian and the wandering Navajo, the ancient Maya, and the surviving Aztec. They are all involved at every moment in their old, struggling religion.

Until they break in a kind of hopelessness under our cheerful, triumphant success. Which is what is rapidly happening. The young Indians who have been to school for many years are losing their religion, becoming discontented, bored, and rootless. An Indian with his own religion inside him *cannot* be bored. The flow of the mystery is too intense all the time . . . .

My criticisms of *The Plumed Serpent* are explicitly of it as a novel. I have always found it hard to get through and myself, in my attempts, an uninspired reader, suffering a great deal of boredom. I have tended to resent, as I turn over the pages, a great redundance of detailed evocation of ritual, and have found myself paying little or no attention to the pages containing the Hymns. And yet I see that, in relation to the clear intention that informs the book, Lawrence had reason for evoking in detail the process, as Ramón-Lawrence imagined and conceived it, by which the old religion might be revived. *The Plumed Serpent*, as thought, is neither irrelevant nor redundant in relation to those basic works, *Psychoanalysis and the Unconscious*, *Fantasia of the Unconscious*, *Study of Thomas Hardy*, and *Introduction to these Paintings*.

It is, of coure, a novel, and, as such, it makes one recall what Lawrence said about the dialogues of Plato: it represents a mode of thought that Lawrence, when he decided that he must spend himself on *The Plumed Serpent*, found necessary—hence his judgment, the book completed, that it was his 'most important thing so far'. It is not, all the same, the equivalent of a Platonic dialogue; it is a novel by a great novelist. It contains abundant evidence of the great creative writer who wrote it; and in the course of my recent re-readings I have filled a large part of a notebook with felicities of thought-formulation that belong distinctively to a novelist's creativity and that one would wish to have ready in one's mind to use.

Nevertheless I am sure that one ought to challenge Lawrence's 'my most important thing so far'. It is of one's immeasurable indebtedness to him that, by thrown-off suggestion, by his expository treatises, and such work in its diversity of modes, as well as by his completely creative (or created) work, he prompts and nourishes one's thinking about the nature of thought and art. The appropriate recognition of the debt, I am convinced, must be—after a due pondering of the complexities, the delicacies, and the ambiguities—to come out with the clear judgment that the 'most important thing' is the greatest novel. After all, 'Art-speech is the only speech' means something. *Women in Love*, which is inclusive, cogent and concrete in the treatment of the complex Laurentian theme, is a better work of art than *The Plumed Serpent*, and the superiority as art is superiority as thought —which amounts to greater cogency.

The reasons I have given already for judging *The Plumed Serpent* unsatisfactory tend to the enforcing of that conclusion. Before going on to discuss *Women in Love*, I will make briefly some other adverse comments on the later novel. It starts and ends with Kate, and she is the one character of major intrinsic interest, the one major personal value, in it. Ramón is adequate to his role, but, as we have him, his complexities and under-currents lie in his past; he has come to his firm decisions before Kate meets him. And actually she is, not only in the effect on the reader, but in the essential creative intention that informs the book, betrayingly the central, most potent and most important person in it. I say 'betrayingly', because Lawrence, in his charged and effective apprehension of the need to make her that, makes inescapable the conclusion that Ramón, in his literary allocution to Cipriano about Wotan, Druids and mistletoe, the Tuatha De Danaan and the rest, is to be taken—though we can't imagine Lawrence really meaning Ramón's cultured silliness—as speaking for the author himself. For, while we are not allowed to doubt that Lawrence's concern for Mexico is intrinsic and intense, neither does the 'art-speech' of *The Plumed Serpent* leave it possible to doubt that when—as author of that just-completed novel—he judges it the most important thing he has so far done, his own sense of the significance of Kate's at last consenting to marry Cipriano and become Malintzi, a goddess, is expressed through Ramón. For Ramón-Lawrence the establishing of the 'worth-whileness' (which, clearly, we are to take as, in terms of *The Plumed Serpent*, success) of Ramón's anti-Catholic anti-crusade is to affect us as being Kate's long-deferred arrival at 'conviction'—the 'conviction' that enables her to marry the Indian Mexican general, and sit ritually by his side as his goddess-wife in a paganized Spanish church.

I put 'conviction' in inverted commas, because it seems to me that few serious readers of Lawrence could be convinced by it— none at all who realized that Kate's presence and involvement represent Lawrence's way of persuading himself that the Birkin-Ursula problem is directly and adequately involved in the single-minded Ramón's religious enterprise, and that *The Plumed Serpent* has the immediacy and completeness of relevance to the essential Laurentian theme that it actually hasn't.

Kate Leslie is forty, has been twice married, and is no longer 'in love with love'. She is a potent presence all through the book— one of Lawrence's formidable middle-aged women, like Mrs Witt of *St Mawr*. Kate is European, very intelligent, sophisticated and more intellectual than Mrs Witt, but, like Mrs Witt's, her formidableness is inseparable from the intensity with which she feels the void and can't forget the unanswerable 'What for?— what ultimately for?' Mexico horrifies her, but dread of 'the thing called life' by the civilized world makes her postpone her departure and resist the impulse to go back to England and Europe.

Lawrence's art conveys with great power her hesitations and her very credible revulsions against remaining in Mexico. It is not till the end of the novel that she allows herself to be married to Cipriano, so becoming qualified to sit by him as Malintzi in religious ceremonies. Cipriano is pure Indian and an ambitious Mexican general—whom she doesn't propose to live with. Nor is her deification accompanied by any credible conviction in her; and Lawrence's 'art-speech' is powerless to convince us that her like—and she is very livingly evoked—could ever have been brought to marry the 'Mexican general' whose devotion to Quetzalcoatl depends on a basically anomalous personal devotion to Ramón—'she knew that without Ramón Cipriano was just an instrument, and not ultimately interesting to her' (page 436).

This last quotation, coming from the novelist in chapter xxv, which is two from the end, betrays that Lawrence endorses Kate's reported reflection. And it is fair to say that he insists that the Ursula–Birkin problem *is*, not only essentially involved, but really dealt with in *The Plumed Serpent*. The insistence takes the form of a tense exchange between Kate and Ramón's new second wife, Teresa.

'I am sorry if I was rude,' she said.
'No', said Kate. 'Apparently it is I who am wrong.'
'Yes, I think you are,' said Teresa. 'You think there is only love. Love is only such a little bit.'
'And what is the rest?'
'How can I tell you, if you do not know? —But do you think Ramón is no more to me than a lover?'
'A husband!' said Kate.
'Ah!' Teresa put her head aside with an odd impatience. 'Those little words! Those little words! Nor either a husband. —He is my life' (page 437).

There is more. But my comment can only be that Lawrence can, 'in imagination', solve the Ursula–Birkin problem very easily in Mexico—so easily that the show of its being dealt with in *The Plumed Serpent* as inseparable from the theme of that book can't be taken at all seriously.

My final criticism is prompted by a phrase I use with a pejorative implication in my last sentence (hence the inverted commas): 'in imagination'. Laurentian imagination, of course, is concerned intensely for the real, being an indispensable mode of the intelligence that explores and tests experience with a view to establishing what the real, for our best insight and apprehension, is. Lawrence's judging *The Plumed Serpent* his 'most important thing' is a disconcerting aberration, but a not incomprehensible one. He felt that in tackling boldly and responsibly the recognized Mexican problem, the newspaper actuality, he was giving Laurentian insight and thought an authority it couldn't otherwise have had. But those most truly appreciative of his distinctive intelligence can't but be aware of the element of *un*realism inescapably entailed in the theme of *The Plumed Serpent*—the theme as developed in the way that makes the book, to Lawrence's sense, so 'important'.

Is it really credible that in actuality Ramón's drive could have had as much success as the novel represents it as having? We note that when the Quetzalcoatl campaign is brought to our attention it is already well advanced; it has an efficient, complex and embracing organization it can depend on, and we are shown, or told, nothing that explains how the establishment of such an organization was possible. There were difficulties enough within Mexico itself: Ramón recognizes some of them when he reflects: 'His people would betray him, he knew that' (page 206), and 'Cipriano, whenever he was away on his own for a time, slipped back into the inevitable Mexican General, fascinated by the opportunity for furthering his own personal ambition, and imposing his own personal will' (page 271). But Mexico was not isolated or insulated; Ramón couldn't realistically count on its remaining for long immune from outside interference.

I will say no more on this head; I will merely add to my adverse criticism this general observation: 'important', used by Lawrence in the way he uses it in his evaluative placing of *The Plumed Serpent*, is a betraying word. It means that even Lawrence can be in a sense a victim of the absence of any sharp boundary between his discursive thought and his fully creative art.

III

'WOMEN IN LOVE'

I HAVE been treating *The Plumed Serpent* as a foil to *Women in Love*, though it is more than that suggests. The author's genius is apparent in it; it has positive Laurentian value, as it would have necessarily to have if it was to serve as a real critical aid. It is not, that is, a foil as being null, or a mere creative failure. Lawrence was attempting the impossible—like Ramón (who says it of himself). But it is a critically invaluable foil to the much greater novel, the achieved 'most important thing'.

Like *The Plumed Serpent*, *Women in Love* starts by evoking a distinctly feminine sense of things; but there is a radical difference—a difference answering to the contrast between the two titles. Kate Leslie, twice married and her much-loved second husband dead, is forty, and through (she knows) with love. Though, as I have said, she affects us as the most potent presence— the potent immediate presence—all through the novel, she remains external to the religious theme till almost the end. In the very last chapter she demonstrates that her own 'Laurentian' problem is related only externally to Ramón's religious preoccupation.

'It is time Cipriano should come home,' said Teresa. But this made Kate rise from her seat with sudden impatience. She would not have this put over her! She would break free, and show them!

The thought that makes her surrender is:

And then what! To sit in a London drawingroom, and add another to all the grimalkins?

But the sisters are young, though experienced—experienced enough to feel the life-problem as pregnant, urgent and menacing. After an opening paragraph of six lines, we have a long conversation in which troubling doubts are raised and more make themselves felt—a conversation which starts: 'Ursula,' said Gudrun, 'don't you *really want* to get married?' We are told of her a page later that she had just come back from London, where she had spent several years working at an art-school as a student, and living a studio life.

'I was hoping now for a man to come along,' Gudrun said, suddenly catching her underlip between her teeth, and making a strange grimace, half sly smiling, half anguish. Ursula was afraid.
'So you have come home, expecting him here?' she laughed.
'Oh my dear,' cried Gudrun, strident. 'I wouldn't go out of my way to look for him. But if there did happen to come along a highly attractive individual of sufficient means—well—' she tailed off ironically. Then she looked searchingly at Ursula, as if to probe her. 'Don't you find yourself getting bored?' she asked of her sister. 'Don't you find that things fail to materialize? *Nothing materializes!* Everything withers in the bud.'
'What withers in the bud?' asked Ursula.
'Oh, everything—oneself—things in general.' There was a pause, while each sister vaguely considered her fate.
'It does frighten one,' said Ursula, and again there was a pause. 'But do you hope to get anywhere by just marrying?'
'It seems to be the inevitable next step,' said Gudrun.

We have already registered a difference between the sisters, though they both testify to the void, the problem, left when individuality is so developed that the established routine of mating and marriage doesn't meet the case. Both Ursula and Gudrun are notably attractive women who, at twenty-six and twenty-five, have had considerable experience of love—experience which, where Ursula is concerned, has its record in *The Rainbow*.

It is made plain in that first chapter that *Women in Love*, as art and thought, is going to be a very different work from *The Plumed Serpent*. Lawrence in both is impelled by a troubled concern for the survival of civilized humanity, but after that opening it is impossible to suppose that in *Women in Love* the Laurentian emphasis on the vitally essential but terribly difficult relation between the fully individual man and the fully individual woman is going to be external and marginal to some ostensibly more embracing theme, as it *is* in *The Plumed Serpent*.

The marvellous economy necessary to the truly embracing completeness of the thought in Lawrence's greatest novel has its effect on us at once in that superbly Laurentian opening chapter.

The conversation between the sisters lapses into painfully embarrassed silence, and, to escape from the intolerable situation, Gudrun, whose cheek, we are told, 'was flushed with repressed emotion', breaks into speech again:

'Shall we go out and look at that wedding?' she asked at length, in a voice that was too casual.

'Yes!' cried Ursula, too eagerly, throwing aside her sewing and leaping up, as if to escape something, thus betraying the tension of the situation and causing a friction of dislike to go over Gudrun's nerves.

They walk through Beldover, a small colliery town of the industrial Midlands, and so the theme of the more-than-economic consequences for civilization of 'economic growth' enters into the pregnant unity of Lawrence's thought—which so wonderfully enforces his aphorism: 'Art-speech is the only speech.' Screened by foliage and the Grammar School fives court in the grounds contiguous to the churchyard, the sisters watch the socially distinguished people arrive. We share the impressions made on the young women by the persons who are going to count in the novel, and it is extraordinary how enthralling to us Lawrence's art makes the narrative. The enthrallingness is inseparable from apprehended significance that promises to develop and increase in pregnancy; Lawrence's genius is that of a supremely great novelist—which is to say that his art is thought and his thought art.

How indisputably he had the right to make his comment on a *A Passage to India*:

Life is more interesting in its undercurrents than in its obvious, and E. M. does see people, people and nothing but people ad nauseam.

What in Mrs Crich, Gerald and Hermione Roddice arrests the attention of the watching sisters is a matter of undercurrents. The external peculiarities are arresting because of the significance they proclaim or suggest, as those perceptive watchers are aware. The suggestive felicities of observation, of course, are the novelist's, whose 'awareness' transcends that of either of the sisters: he can sensitize the reader's apprehension for the play of interacting 'undercurrents' that is to ensue. In fact, without a jolt, without any disturbing suggestion of a shift, he can develop and supplement the sisters' insights with illuminating commentaries they certainly couldn't themselves have supplied. The most notable instance in the opening chapter concerns Hermione Roddice—whose observable peculiarities of appearance, bearing and behaviour are so very striking.

People were silent when she passed, impressed, roused, wanting to jeer, yet for some reason silenced. Her long, pale face, that she carried lifted up, somewhat in the Rossetti fashion, seemed almost drugged, as if a strange mass of thoughts coiled in the darkness within her, and she was never allowed to escape.

Ursula watched her with fascination. She knew her a little. She was the most remarkable woman in the Midlands. Her father was a Derbyshire Baronet of the old school, she was a woman of the new school, full of intellectuality and heavy, nerve-worn consciousness. She was passionately interested in reform, her soul was given up to the public cause. But she was a man's woman, it was the manly world that held her.

*　　*　　*

Hermione knew herself to be well-dressed; she knew herself to be the social equal, if not far the superior, of anyone she was likely to meet in Willey Green. She knew she was accepted in the world of culture and of intellect. . . . No one could put her down, no one could make a mock of her, because she stood among the first, and those that were against her were below her, either in rank, or in wealth, or in high association of thought and progress and understanding. All her life she had sought to make herself invulnerable, unassailable, beyond reach of the world's judgment.

And yet her soul was tortured, exposed.

And she so wanted someone to close up this deficiency, to close it up for ever. She craved for Rupert Birkin. When he was there, she felt complete, she was sufficient, whole. For the rest of the time she was established on the sand, built over a chasm . . .

*　　*　　*

And this conjunction with her, which was his highest fulfilment also, with the perverseness of a wilful child he wanted to deny. With the wilfulness of an obstinate child, he wanted to break the holy connection that was between them.

He would be at the wedding: he was to be groom's man. He would be in the church waiting.

There is a good deal more about Hermione and her relation to Birkin, but we have no sense of any redundancy. It all seems to issue organically out of the sisters' actual perceptions, and is found later to have prepared us for scenes and episodes that develop Lawrence's thought and novelistic art—which are one (a truth potently exemplified in the opening chapter).

The marriage-union solemnized in the church is a conventional one—and conventionally 'normal', serving as that to set off the problem, seeming to them insoluble, that troubles the two sisters. What, regarding them and their respective different fates, we note as significant in terms of the Laurentian thought-movement of the novel, is their identifying among socially distinguished persons attending the wedding-ceremony Gerald Crich and Rupert Birkin. 'Ursula,' we are told, 'was left thinking about Birkin. He piqued her, attracted her and annoyed her. She wanted to know him more.' Her interest in him is insisted on in a way we recognize as significant. And the chapter ends with this:

Gerald Crich came, fair, goodlooking, healthy, with a great reserve of energy. He was erect and complete, there was a strange stealth glistening through his amiable, almost happy appearance. Gudrun rose sharply and went away. She could not bear it. She wanted to be alone, to know this strange, sharp inoculation that had changed the whole temper of her blood.

There are many diversities of relation between woman and man coming under the head of 'love'. In the opening chapter of *Women in Love* the playing-off of the Gudrun–Gerald relation against the Ursula–Birkin relation, which counts for so much in the structure and significance of the novel, starts. An expository offer such as this must proceed by concentration on selected places: in any case, a branching-out and a referring back and forward will occur, since the closely organized—the organic— whole imagined and conceived entails a local pregnancy. I will, then, move to the fourth chapter, 'Diver', which, in its ostensible limited self, is comparatively simple.

On a showery morning in spring when the black-thorn is out, Gudrun and Ursula, freed from school (it is Saturday), go for a walk, and are approaching Willey Water. In front of them, near the road, is a boat-house and a little landing-stage.

Suddenly, from the boat-house, a white figure ran out, frightening in its swift sharp transit, across the old landing-stage. It launched in a white arc through the air, there was a bursting of the water, and among the smooth ripples a swimmer was making out to space, in a centre of faintly heaving motion. The whole otherworld, wet and remote, he had to himself. He could move into the pure translucency of the grey, uncreated water.

The penultimate word of that passage, 'uncreated', has a special Laurentian sense. Like that of all great creative writers, his creativity manifests itself in new shades of suggestion, new felicities of force, got out of the common language—in (we feel) an inspired way, rather than by calculating intention. But 'uncreated' is one of the words regarding which, however the special use first occurred to Lawrence, we know that in such a use it represents a deliberate and conscious decision to make it serve as a quasi-technical Laurentian term. I can say this because the prefixing of 'uncreated' to 'water' requires an explanation, and the explanation involves an account of the underlying distinctive and original thought.

Since Laurentian thought is a unity, a coherent organic and comprehensive totality, anything *ad hoc* answering to the word 'account' is out of the question. What is wanted is a sufficient hint at the bearing (this being important) of 'uncreated' on Gerald's case, and on the significance of the 'outburst' triggered off in Gudrun by the sight of him swimming and on the question of why Ursula should have found such intensity of response incomprehensible. I will hark back, then, to an exchange which takes place, towards the end of the second chapter, 'Shortlands', between Gerald and Birkin, conversing apart at the wedding-reception:

'You don't believe in having any standard of behaviour at all, do you?' he challenged Birkin censoriously.

'Standard—no. I hate standards. But they're necessary for the common ruck. Anybody who is anything can just be himself, and do as he likes.'

'But what do you mean by being himself?' said Gerald. 'Is that an aphorism or a cliché?'

'I mean it's just doing what you want to do. I think it was perfect good form in Laura to bolt from Lupton at the church door. It was almost a masterpiece in good form. It's the hardest thing in the world to act spontaneously on one's impulses—and it's the only really gentlemanly thing to do—provided you're fit to do it.'

'You don't expect me to take you seriously, do you?' asked Gerald.

'Yes, Gerald, you're one of the very few people I do expect that of.'

'Then I'm afraid I can't come up to your expectations here, at any rate. You think people should just do as they like.'

'I think they always do. But I should like them to like the purely individual thing in themselves, which makes them act in singleness. And they only like to do the collective thing.'

What's involved here, in the point and meaning of what Birkin says, is the force of three words in particular: individual, spontaneous, singleness. You'll recall the way in which Lawrence identifies life with individuality, and my own proposition, advanced and enforced (I hope) in the chapter on *Little Dorrit* in *Dickens the Novelist*, that life is there only in the individual being— a truism that makes Lawrence's point in a form adapted to my critical purpose. No equivalent proposition applies to electricity, which is a general force; it presents no such unamenableness to statistical, mathematical, quantitative or, in sum, general treatment as life does. 'Life', as I've said more than once, *is* a necessary word; that is, it's far from meaningless, and Lawrence, making his necessary points, has to use it—and uses it without inner resistance. 'Nothing,' his maxim runs, 'is important but life.'

One can speak significantly—one has to do in persuading one's thought to go on unfolding—of the development of life. As, then, life develops and advances towards man and *in* man it seeks to purify, to single out (in a special sense of that phrasal verb) the individuality of the individual; to attain to being pre-eminently *there* in the complete, and completely 'single' human being. When Birkin says, 'It's the hardest thing in the world to act spontaneously on one's impulses—and it's the only really gentlemanly thing to do—provided you're fit to do it,' Gerald does, I think, vaguely know what he means. The 'impulses' in question are not those of the ego and its personal will; they come from the spontaneity of one who has achieved singleness, and can act out of his whole unified being.

Lawrence somewhere compares the individual life to a mountain tarn that is fed from below, no inlet being perceptible. The promptings of true spontaneity—those, for instance, in which the creativity of an artist are manifested—come from the hidden source, which 'it's the hardest thing in the world' to learn how to draw from. Lawrence in his discursive treatises, *Psychoanalysis and the Unconscious*, makes plain why he treats the hidden source as the access to the real and profound authority that may properly be called religious, and why, in his diagnosis of a sick world, he makes indifference to the source the lethal malady—a blankness inherent in technologico-Benthamism—that will destroy our civilization.

'Uncreated', in the sense in which Lawrence uses it, applies to living individuals. He applies it to the empty lostness in the eyes of Mexican Indians—to their having stopped short of 'manhood' (to use Ramón's word) and their obvious helplessness to achieve it. 'Manhood' entails the completeness that manifests itself in responsibility—the responsibility that 'fits' one to 'act spontaneously on one's impulses'.

Lawrence actually, in the sentence in question, calls, not Gerald, but the water 'uncreated'; that, however, doesn't prevent our realizing that the essential purpose of the sentence is to imply something about Gerald's case, and its representative quality. I had better quote it again, with the previous sentence:

The whole otherworld, wet and remote, he had to himself. He could move into the pure translucency of the grey, uncreated water.

If we have read before through *Women in Love*, we realize that the end is here prefigured—the lapsing out from life of Gerald, undirected energy now, since he has nothing else to be, in the skiers' Tyrolese snow-world. The prefiguring renders in 'art-speech' the inevitability with which technologico-Benthamite civilization moves towards the end which is imaged in Gerald's. Ursula and Gudrun have not read *Women in Love*; hence the mutual incomprehension that attends on their differing reactions to the sight of Gerald swimming:

Gudrun stood by the stone wall, watching, 'How I envy him,' she said, in low, desirous tones.
'Ugh!' shivered Ursula. 'So cold!'
'Yes, but how good, how really fine, to swim out there!'

*   *   *

THOUGHT, WORDS AND CREATIVITY

'Don't you wish it were you?' asked Gudrun, looking at Ursula.
'I do,' said Ursula. 'But I'm not sure—it's so wet.'

'No,' said Gudrun, reluctantly. ... She stood motionless gazing
over the water at the face which washed up and down on the flood,
as he swam steadily. From his separate element he saw them, and he
exulted to himself because of his own advantage, his possession of a
world to himself. He was immune and perfect.

* * *

He was alone now, alone and immune in the middle of the waters,
which he had all to himself. He exulted in his isolation in the new
element, unquestioned and unconditioned. He was happy, thrusting
with his legs and all his body, without bond or connection anywhere,
just himself in the watery world.

Gudrun envied him almost painfully. Even this momentary possession of pure isolation and fluidity seemed to be so terribly desirable
that she felt herself as if damned, out there on the high-road.

'God, what it is to be a man!' she cried.

'What?' exclaimed Ursula in surprise.

'The freedom, the liberty, the mobility!' cried Gudrun, strangely
flushed and brilliant. 'You're a man, you want to do a thing, you do
it. You haven't the *thousand* obstacles a woman has in front of her'.
Ursula wondered what was in Gudrun's mind, to occasion this outburst. She could not understand.

'What do you want to do?' she asked.

'Nothing,' cried Gudrun in swift repudiation. 'But supposing I did.
It is impossible, it is one of the impossibilities of life, for me to take
my clothes off now and simply jump in. But isn't it ridiculous, doesn't
it simply prevent our living?'

She was so hot, so flushed, so furious, that Ursula was puzzled.

The sisters know Gerald as the formidably masculine man who
has, as a 'Napoleon of industry' (Birkin's not altogether innocent
phrase), revolutionized the Crich mines, raising them to a high
and pitiless efficiency. They are soon to witness a demonstration
of the will exerted in the achievement. The will and the energy
go with the blond good looks and the poised superiority that
make him attractive to Gudrun. Nevertheless, both of the sisters,
different as they are, note something about the energy in a way
that implies criticism. As they proceed further alongside Willey
Water, they get a view of 'Shortlands', the Crich family house,
and Gudrun, admiring, says 'It has form, too', and specifies:

'Wordsworth and Jane Austen.'

Ursula laughed.

'Don't you think so?' repeated Gudrun.

'Perhaps. But I don't think the Criches fit the period. I know Gerald is putting in a private electric plant, for lighting the house, and is making all kinds of latest improvements.'

Gudrun shrugged her shoulders swiftly. 'Of course,' she said, 'That's quite inevitable.'

'Quite,' laughed Ursula. 'He's several generations of youngness at one go. They hate him for it. He takes them all by the scruff of the neck, and fairly flings them along. He'll have to die soon, when he's made every possible improvement, and there will be nothing more to improve. He's got *go*, anyhow.'

'Certainly he's got go,' said Gudrun. 'In fact I've never seen a man who showed signs of so much. The unfortunate thing is, where does his *go* go to, what becomes of it.'

'Oh, I know,' said Ursula. 'It goes in applying the latest appliances'.

'Exactly,' said Gudrun.'

Gudrun seems severer in her critical attitude towards Gerald, but it is Gudrun who is attracted by him. The difference between the sisters is in fact radical—how radical comes out, a little further on in their walk, when they have encountered Hermione Roddice, who reminds them in her patrician *de haut en bas* manner that they have been invited to Breadalby. Gudrun's refusal to share, or to understand, Ursula's indignant recoil from Hermione takes the form of an essentially edged and snubbing coldness. The difference is as important in Lawrence's thought as the difference between Gerald and Birkin.

It is important, too, that Gudrun should be, in a minor way, an artist: when we look into the justice and significance of the qualification, 'in a minor way', we find that we are considering the nature, and the disastrous end, of her relations, with Gerald.

But *difference*. When, having seen Birkin's car outside the school (he is an inspector), Hermione, with characteristic *sans gêne*, seeks him out in the class-room (chapter III is called that). Birkin has been a wholly sympathetic advisory presence at Ursula's botany lesson on hazel catkins, the aim being to impress on the children's memory the difference between the male and the female. Hermione says to Ursula about Gudrun, whom she has met in London in the social world where intellectuals and artists count:

'I think some of her work is really wonderful. I have two water-wagtails, carved in wood, and painted—perhaps you have seen it?'
'No,' said Ursula.
'I think it is perfectly wonderful—like a flash of instinct.'
'Her little carvings *are* strange,' said Ursula.
'Perfectly beautiful—full of primitive passion—'

To which Ursula, who naturally knows her sister better than Hermione does, responds with this:

'Isn't it queer that she always likes little things?—she must always work small things, that one can put between one's hands, birds and tiny animals. She likes to look through the wrong end of the opera glasses, and see the world in that way—why is it, do you think?'

The context, which is in its turn confirmed by what it picks up from the preceding pages of the book, confirms one's immediate recognition that the last sentence—which ends with a question-mark, is implicitly, and at least not altogether unconsciously, critical of Gudrun. In any case, the datum sufficiently explicit in small things 'that one can put between one's hands' goes to explain why her envy of Gerald's 'freedom' to do what he wants should have been so extravagantly intense. 'He was happy ... without bond or connection anywhere; just himself ...'; 'immune and perfect.'

There is an illusion involved, of course, for the exultation depends on a sense of superiority:

From his separate element he saw them, and he exulted to himself because of his own advantage, his possession of a world to himself. ... He could see the girls watching from outside, and that pleased him.

His freedom is freedom of the ego; power, that is, to indulge the will that belongs to the ego. That is the freedom Gudrun so intensely desires for herself. She, of course, is something that Gerald is not—an artist, but fated to be inescapably only a minor one. 'Thank God, I am not free any more than a rooted tree is free': that is the utterance of a great artist. Even the carved water-wagtails were the creative product of something other than ego and will. But Gudrun hasn't deep and strong rooting. She isn't—to change from one Laurentian way of putting things to another—a profoundly unified totality of life, and can't, for creativity, draw freely on the deep-lying source.

The relation of art to life, or the place of art *in* life, figures inevitably in the explicit thought of *Women in Love*, and the significance of Gudrun in respect of that theme is brought out fully in the daunting close of the novel. The scene is the lonely winter-sports hostel in the snow-world of the high Tyrol. Among the guests is Loerke, the gnome-like German sculptor. Birkin says of him to Gerald—both of them find him repulsive: 'He's a gnawing little negation, gnawing at the roots of life.' But to Gudrun, who is much impressed by what she has been told about the great granite frieze which he is doing for a great granite factory in Cologne, and has talked with him about sculpture,

'there was in Loerke the rock-bottom of all life.'—'In the last issue he cared about nothing, he troubled about nothing, he made not the slightest attempt to be at one with anything. He existed a pure, un-connected will . . .'

In short, he believed in nothing, and was perfectly free from the burden of felt life-responsibility. One has to conclude, though Gudrun clearly doesn't, that if her account of Loerke is right, he can certainly not, however favourably she is impressed by him, be a greater artist than she is.

At any rate, though he is confidently assertive, he doesn't bother to be intelligent. This is his way of answering questions of Gudrun's about the frieze:

'Art should *interpret* industry, as art once interpreted religion.'
'But does your fair interpret industry?' she asked him.
'Certainly. What is man doing, when he is at a fair like this? He is fulfilling the counterpart of labour—the machine works him, instead of he the machine. He enjoys the mechanical motion, in his own body.'

The frieze as he describes it is a representation of drunken members of the *lumpen-proletariat* giving themselves up clownishly to the mechanized pleasures of a fair.

Gudrun takes to Loerke; 'something in Gudrun', we are told, 'seemed to accord with him'. He liked talking with her, and he wouldn't talk in the presence of the men; but he preferred Ursula to be there, as a sort of transmitter to Gudrun. 'Transmitter' means that Ursula's German was better than Gudrun's, for to him she was merely instrumental; but the preference turned out to be unfortunate for Loerke. It led to a demonstration he hadn't foreseen of a difference between the sisters he hadn't, in his conscious self-sufficiency, done justice to. Actually, the manner of his response to the demonstration proved the self-sufficiency to be largely illusion. 'Do you do nothing but architectural sculpture?' Gudrun asked him one evening. Perhaps the question betrayed a vague sense in Gudrun that Loerke's talk about architectural sculpture, and the relation of art to life, had hardly been thought. However that might be, the consequence of the question and Ursula's presence was to elicit from Loerke a second account of art, one inconsistent with the first. In answer to Gudrun he produced 'a photogravure reproduction of a statuette signed F. Loerke'.

The statuette was of a naked girl, small, finely made, sitting on a great naked horse. The girl was young and tender, a mere bud. She was sitting sideways on the horse, her face in her hands, as if in shame and grief, in a little abandon. Her hair, which was short and must be flaxen, fell forward, divided, half covering her hands.

Her limbs were young and tender. Her legs, scarcely formed yet, the legs of a maiden just passing towards cruel womanhood, dangled childishly over the side of the powerful horse, pathetically, the small feet folded one over the other, as if to hide. But there was no hiding. . . .

The horse stood stock still, stretched in a kind of start. It was a massive, magnificent stallion, rigid with pent-up power. Its neck was arched and terrible, like a sickle, its flanks were pressed back, rigid with power.

Gudrun went pale, and a darkness came over her eyes, like shame, she looked up with a certain supplication, almost slave-like.

She doesn't, however, admit the effect on her—even, it seems, to herself—or the notion of art implicit in such an effect. She tries to hide the signs of her disturbed state in an ostensibly cool sculptor-to-sculptor exchange about the size and substance of the statuette depicted in the photogravure. Loerke, of course, is not deceived; he knows well enough the nature of her impressed-ness—it is what he wanted. 'He closed his eyes and looked aside, triumphant.' The impulse to challenge him is absent in Gudrun;

that is left to her sister, who *has* the strong indignant impulse, and the courage of it:

'Why,' said Ursula, 'did you make the horse so stiff? It is as stiff as a block.'

'Stiff?' he repeated, in arms at once.

'Yes. *Look* how stock and stupid and brutal it is. Horses are sensitive, quite delicate and sensitive, really.'

He raised his shoulder, spread his hands in a shrug of slow indifference, as much as to inform her she was an amateur and an impertinent nobody.

'Wissen Sie', he said, with an insulting patience and condescension in his voice, 'that horse is a certain *form*, part of a whole form. It is part of a work of art, a piece of form. It is not a picture of a friendly horse to which you give a lump of sugar, do you see—it is part of a work of art, it has no relation to anything outside that work of art.'

Ursula, angry at being treated quite so insultingly *de haut en bas*, from the height of esoteric art to the depth of general exoteric amateurism, replied hotly, lifting her face:

'But it *is* a picture of a horse, nevertheless.'

He lifted his shoulders in another shrug.

'As you like—it is not a picture of a cow, certainly.'

Here Gudrun broke in, flushed and brilliant, anxious to avoid any more of this, any more of Ursula's persistence in giving herself away.

It is herself, however, that Gudrun gives away, for in her castigation of Ursula she takes a line that is contradicted by Loerke on the same page—without either artist noticing the contradiction. She rebukes Ursula for objecting to Loerke's horse because it doesn't represent *her* idea of one: there is, she asserts, 'another idea altogether, quite another'. Ursula's persistence in refusing to be bullied into denying what she sees and knows triggers off Loerke's launch into the incompatible account of art—which is nonsensical too, for it is Clive Bell's 'significant form', the sophisticated fatuity that Lawrence dispatches with such witty conclusiveness in *Introduction to these Paintings*:[1]

'But why does he have this idea of a horse?' she said. 'I know it is his idea. I know it is a picture of himself, really—'

Loerke snorted with rage.

'A picture of myself!' he repeated in derision. 'Wissen sie, gnädige

[1] *Phoenix I*, p. 551 ff.; paperback, p. 143 ff.

Frau, that is a Kunstwerk, a work of art. It is a work of art, it is a picture of nothing, of absolutely nothing. It has nothing to do with anything but itself, it has no relation with the everyday world of this and other, there is no connection between them, absolutely none, they are two different and distinct planes of existence . . . .'

Gudrun, as if showing hostility to Ursula were the principle at issue, joins in, by way of reinforcing Loerke's attack on her. But Ursula isn't to be bullied into silence:

'It isn't a word of it true of all this harangue you have made me,' she replied flatly. 'The horse is a picture of your own stock, stupid brutality, and the girl was a girl you loved and tortured and then ignored.'

★　★　★

'As for your world of art and your world of reality, . . . you have to separate the two, because you can't bear to realize what a stock, stiff, hide-bound brutality you are really, so you say "it's the world of art." The world of art is only the truth about the real world, that's all—but you are too far gone to see it.'

Gudrun betrays her undersense that Ursula is right about Loerke and the statuette by asking in a voice that was quite cool and casual, as if resuming a casual conversation:

'Was the girl a model?'
'Nein, sie war kein Modell. Sie war eine kleine Malschülerin.'
'An art-student!' replied Gudrun.
And how the situation revealed itself to her! She saw the girl art-student . . . and Loerke, the well-known master-sculptor, and the girl probably well-brought up, and of good family, thinking herself so great to be his mistress. Oh how well she knew the common callousness of it all. Dresden, Paris or London, what did it matter? She knew it.'

She doesn't, however, convey to Ursula that she was right about Loerke, or cease to find him a man whose company she enjoys; nor does Loerke himself abstain, in talk with Gerald, who at this point comes in, from implicitly confirming—without apparent consciousness of exposing himself—what actually amounts to Ursula's reading of the human significance of the statuette.

There is more that bears—in direct explicitness—on the relation of art to life in the closing pages of *Women in Love*. But I have dealt with the theme fully enough—it had to be in some detail—to make my point: the close attention Lawrence pays to differing attitudes towards art serves—is inseparable from—his concern to bring out the significance of the death, which occurs towards the very end of the book, of Gerald, lapsed out into the all-covering snow. I think we may fairly say that Lawrence intends us to identify with his own Ursula's attitude and her conclusion: 'The world of art is only the truth about the real world, that's all . . .'

Her phrase, 'the truth about the real world', obviously covers the intention of the Laurentian maxim: 'Nothing is important but life.' Of course, Ursula is not a genius, and isn't capable of the context of penetrating and comprehensive thought that justifies Lawrence's: 'Art-speech is the only speech'. It is not enough, however, to stop at saying this. One must go on to say that the full justifying meaning, the enforcement, of the maxim is to be found in the art-which-is-thought of the marvellously organic and comprehensive totality which is *Women in Love*.

Such a work is inexhaustibly complex and pregnant. I have made plain the spirit of my approach to it by the emphasis I have laid on 'thought' and the way in which I have used that word. Such an approach, I think, is in no way arbitrary, but it can't proceed by anything like a simple forward-moving commentary on unfolding 'plot'. I must, then, go back now to consider Gerald's case—and he is very much (inverted commas now) a 'case'—at the time of his confident plunge into Willey Water and of Gudrun's ecstatically furious envy of the 'freedom' he enjoys. It is significant, in relation to the part played by Gudrun in his self-destruction, that she, the envier, should have been the one to say, taking up the point from Ursula, 'The unfortunate thing is, where does his go go to, what becomes of it?' We know that what becomes of it is perfect assimilation to the blank snow-world, and that this represents the fate feared by Lawrence for neo-Benthamite humanity—for humanity that believes in nothing but 'economic growth' and 'welfare'.

The Gerald envied by the Gudrun watching him swimming in Willey Water has energy and efficiency, and the will to use them. The sisters are enabled (unwillingly) to contemplate the nature of the will in what is so vividly evoked in chapter IX,

'Coal-dust'—the episode at the level-crossing, where Gerald, having ridden up to the closed gates on his Arab mare, makes her stay there, he with pitiless resolution controlling the frenzy of her terror, while the long train from the colliery, with a hideous clashing of its buffers, moves slowly by. The two women leave him in no doubt of their horrified disapproval, but he shows surprise at their intensities and doesn't defend the callousness they cry out against—he feels he has no need to, the firmness being necessary.

An equivalent explanation attends on the firmness he shows in face of the miners' hatred—the hatred generated by his ruthless modernization of the mines. My 'ruthless' has its prompting in the episode of the Arab mare, in which she figures very aptly, we recognize, the living sensitiveness of life. In such an undertaking as the modernization of the Crich mines, some insensitiveness is compelled in the efficient exercise of will. With obvious justice we can say that the self-sufficiency Gerald, swimming in Willey Water, exults in—'He exulted in his isolation in the new element, unquestioned and unconditioned'—makes the given insensitiveness natural to him. What Lawrence is intimating is that technologico-Benthamite civilization breeds Gerald's kind of egoism; the egoism that exults in feeling oneself to be self-sufficient, unconditioned and 'immune'—in short, rootless. To say this is not to impute any position to Lawrence that could sound simple in any fair stating of it.

If we want to justify 'ruthless' as applied to Gerald we have only to contrast him with Thomas Crich, his father, from whom he has taken over the command. Thomas Crich thought of himself as a Christian, and his religion was what today is called 'compassion':

He had been so constant to his lights, so constant to charity, and to his love for his neighbour. Perhaps he had loved his neighbour even better than himself—which is going one further than the commandment. Always this flame had burned in his heart, sustaining him through everything, the welfare of the people. He was a large employer of labour, he was great mine-owner. And he had never lost this from his heart, that in Christ he was one with his workmen. Nay, he felt inferior to them, as if they through poverty and labour were nearer to God than he.

Thomas Crich's religion, I have said, was compassion. But 'compassion' as invoked today by Lord Snow and Lord Annan, who are representative or nothing, is a word that suggests no religious context. Nevertheless, the enlightened, in their use of it, descend directly from Thomas Crich. And the ethic of compassion, as Lawrence in a number of places points out, or rather assumes that no one will question, descends directly from what had become in the early stages of the progressive West a dominant strand in the Christian tradition.

Lawrence, we know, is convinced that no positive acceptance, no 'belief', however strongly based in cultural habit, can be adequate to sustain a civilization, or even an individual being, that is not at bottom essentially religious—that doesn't, that is, keep unforgettably present for recognition the need to transcend all egoistic satisfactions and aims. Lawrence, of course, had no thought of reviving Thomas Crich's religion. It ignored, and in ignoring, outraged something that has its part in any truly basic, any profound and lastingly satisfying attitude in face of the cosmos. What this something was Lawrence makes plain in the paragraph (page 225) following that from which I quoted last:

And all the while, his wife opposed him like one of the great demons of hell. Strange, like a bird of prey, with the fascinating beauty and abstraction of a hawk, she had beat against the bars of his philanthropy, and, like a hawk in a cage, she had sunk into silence. By force of circumstance, because all the world combined to make the cage unbreakable, he had been too strong for her, he had kept her prisoner. And because she was his prisoner, his passion for her had always remained as keen as death. He had always loved her, loved her with intensity. Within the cage she was denied nothing, she was given all licence. But she had gone almost mad. Of wild and overweening temper, she could not bear the humiliation of her husband's soft, half-appealing kindness to everybody. He was not deceived by the poor. He knew they came and sponged on him . . .

* * *

Sometimes, it seemed to Mrs Crich as if her husband were some subtle funeral bird, feeding on the miseries of the people. It seemed to her he was never satisfied unless there were some sordid tale being poured out to him, which he drank in with a sort of mournful, sympathetic satisfaction. He would have no *raison d'être* if there were no lugubrious miseries in the world, as an undertaker would have no meaning if there were no funerals.

Mrs Crich recoiled back upon herself, she recoiled away from this world of creeping democracy.

Thought and art are triumphantly one in the exposure of Thomas Crich's 'philanthropy' as a dominant mode of egoism in him, a self-centred indulgence belonging to the enclosed ego. The egoism and will are revealed as such in the manner, rendered dramatically, of his clinging to life when plainly dying; and Lawrence's mastery of his art-as-thought is manifested in the impossibility of separating what is in itself expository Laurentian comment from the relevant directly dramatic presentment— almost the impossibility of fixing imaginatively a line between them. Thus we have:

He would die even now without breaking down, without knowing what his feelings were towards her. All his life, he had said: 'Poor Christina, she has such a strong temper.' With unbroken will, he had stood by this position with regard to her, he had substituted pity for all his hostility, pity had been his shield and his safeguard, and his infallible weapon . . . . But now his pity, with his life, was wearing thin, and the dread, almost amounting to horror, was rising into being. But before the armour of his pity really broke, he would die, as an insect when its shell is cracked. This was his final resource. . . . He denied death its victory.

Compassion is his 'armour'. As for Gerald, about whose 'undercurrents' his father's death would reveal new things, one could hardly say of him, in his role of Napoleon of industry, that he accepted the ethics of compassion. Yet 'the plausible ethics of productivity', we must assume, did recommend itself to him, and if you liberate 'compassion', as the current use of the word does, from anything that we can with conviction call 'religious', then what is left to avow is 'the plausible ethics of productivity', with, perhaps, some thin ghost of 'ethical' emotion in attendance.

The phrase comes in chapter V, 'In the Train', which is filled mainly with a conversation between Gerald and Birkin who, having encountered one another fortuitously at the station, travel up to London together. Gerald starts the conversation by quoting something from an article in his *Daily Telegraph*, and before it has got far, we have this:

'So while you get the coal I must chase the rabbit?' said Birkin, mocking at Gerald.

'Something like that,' said Gerald.

Birkin watched him narrowly. He saw the perfectly good-humoured callousness, even strange, glistening malice, in Gerald, glistening through the plausible ethics of productivity.

'Gerald,' he said, 'I rather hate you.'

It is Birkin who insists on what is for him the deep underlying question, raising the theme that is his own insistent preoccupation — 'What for, what ultimately for?', though Gerald doesn't seem to take it very seriously:

'What do you think is the aim and object of your life, Gerald?' he asked.

Again Gerald was taken aback. He could not think what his friend was getting at. Was he poking fun, or not?

'At this moment, I couldn't say off-hand,' he replied, with faintly ironic humour.

'Do you think to live is the be-all and end-all of life?' Birkin asked, with direct and attentive seriousness.

Gerald's responses having made it plain that he has never really considered the question at all, Birkin presses no further, but makes his own self-testing, self-probing avowal: 'I want the finality of love.'

'I don't believe a woman, and nothing but a woman, will ever make my life,' said Gerald.

'Not the centre and core of it — the love between you and a woman?' asked Birkin.

Gerald's eyes narrowed with a queer dangerous smile as he watched the other man.

'I never quite feel it that way,' he said.

'You don't? Then wherein does life centre for you?'

'I don't know — that's what I want somebody to tell me. As far as I can make out, it doesn't centre at all. It is artificially held *together* by the social mechanism.'

That is still a modern answer — the real and unusually intelligent modern answer. And what I want to emphasize is the rightness and supreme importance of the way Lawrence associates — rather, makes inseparably one — the question, or problem, 'What ultimately for?' and the problem of love; or rather, the problem of finding the right answers, the humanly most satisfying answers, to serious self-questioning about the relations between individual women and individual men. It is significant that Lawrence's most complete and most searching inquest into neo-Benthamite civilization should have for title, *Women in Love*. Already, a long half-century ago, he was defending women against the enlightened stupidity that, claiming for them equality with men, offered to reduce them, in proper accord with the Benthamite ethos, to arithmetical human units. Things have got worse since those days, in direct development, and we have reason now to apprehend that detected failure to observe the principle of equality will, like racial discrimination, very soon be punishable by law. Lest this apprehension that the principle will be enforced in its absurdest extremes should be dismissed as itself absurd, I will mention a couple of facts: there is a society at Oxford that aims at legally compelling every college to admit men and women in equal numbers; and, as, listening to the news, we hear the recently established alternation of male and female voices in the announcing, it is brought disconcertingly home to us that 'equality' has had a portentous victory in the world of the BBC.

The sharp neo-Benthamite advance is not merely a menace to the real distinctive status of women as women; it portends lethal consequences for the civilization that endorses (in the name of progress), and suffers, the enlightened development. For, as Lawrence insists, it is properly a question, not of equality and inequality, but of difference, and the difference is essential to human life. It is essential not only in the most obvious way, the continuance of the species depending on it. The difference in that respect carries other respects—other modes of difference—along with it. Neither man nor woman can represent a complete *humanitas*; the close association that is inter-influence and mutual supplementation (and more) is necessary. It is of very little use trying to define the nature of the difference with adjectives—with words in general—that lie handy. Perhaps it is best to stop at saying that it is vital—vital in another sense than the biological. Lawrence's use of the English language as a creative writer goes much further; it does what language can't do when put to expounding discursively with strictly and narrowly explicit logic. This is not to dismiss his discursive expositions (as I must call them), but *they* are Laurentian and unique: they help one, in fact, to be more delicately and fully aware of something characteristic of Lawrence's genius that is always present in his novels and tales. It greatly helps towards a full appreciation of Gerald's fate and its significance to be familiar with Lawrence's criticism of the western cult of love—an idealizing (this he makes plain) which is disastrously falsifying. The criticism has a developed expository expression in a number of places. Of these, what I have re-read most recently—I am excluding, of course, passages that belong to the supreme presentment of Laurentian thought in art—is the essay called 'Love was once a Little Boy', which as I have it is to be found in *Reflections on the Death of a Porcupine*.[1] It is in that essay that Lawrence says: 'Hate is not the opposite of love. The real opposite of love is individuality.' A little further on, after saying that 'we enact a perpetual paradox,' he gives us, in immediate explanation, this:

Take the love of a man and a woman today. As sure as you start with a case of 'true love' between them, you end with a terrific struggle and conflict of the two opposing egos or individualities. It's nobody's fault: it's the inevitable result of trying to snatch an intensified individuality out of the mutual flame.

Further on in the essay we read:

This subtle streaming of desire is beyond the control of the ego. The ego says: 'This is *my* love, to do as I like with! This is my desire, given to me for my own pleasure.'
But the ego deceives itself. The individual cannot possess the love which he himself feels. Neither should he be entirely possessed by it. Neither man nor woman should sacrifice individuality to love; nor love to individuality.
If we lose desire out of our lives, we become empty vessels. But if we break our own integrity, we become a squalid mess, like a jar of honey dropped and smashed.

This leads me to the relation between Birkin and Ursula, and to the chapter (XIX) called 'Moony'. Birkin already, in chapter III, 'Class-room', knows that he is through with Hermione Roddice, and we know, from what we are told in the first chapter by way of interpretive comment on the strikingly odd, the

[1] It is to be found also in *Phoenix II*.

THOUGHT, WORDS AND CREATIVITY

inwardly strained, distinction of the strange woman we see, why he is determined to complete his escape from her, and why she *needs* to hold him clutched. The confirmation—we get it in the class-room, where they break into a savage quarrel before the embarrassed teacher, Ursula—is vividly and convincingly dramatic:

> 'But your passion is a lie,' he went on violently. 'It isn't passion at all, it's your *will*. It's your bullying will. You want to clutch things and have them in your power. And why?'

The answer to the 'why' is what the last sentence of the passage I quoted from Lawrence's essay intimates: 'But if we break our own integrity, we become a squalid mess ...' Breaking our own integrity is what 'perfect love' requires. But the perfection postulated is a mere word, empty of meaning: what the pair of lovers— or one of them—think (or thinks) of 'as perfect' is complete intimacy, the intimacy that would amount to merging. This, if it were achievable—but it isn't, would entail the extinction of both individualities. In actuality, one of the lovers would achieve —for a while, at least, a powerfully clutching possession of the other. But how do you go on clutching a mess? Hermione is a 'case', and her 'case' is desperation that has left her the possession of only will, which it intensifies; a mess is what, as she pursues her undisguised and undisguisable designs on Birkin, she herself dramatically enacts—*is*, for the will doesn't serve any integrated whole.

It is Birkin and Ursula who, as a pair, are played against Gerald and Gudrun (it is, of course, an interplay) in the total thought of *Women in Love*—the thought that completes itself in Gerald's death in the snow-world. Birkin's earlier relations with Hermione are essential, but instrumentally, as helping to present the difficulties he has with Ursula, and so to communicate the full significance of the later pairing, and the nature of the needs that are satisfied—as neither Gerald's nor Gudrun's are. Ursula is decidedly not a 'case'; she is sensitive, perceptive and intelligent, and Birkin feels a strong attraction to her that we, in our turn, feel to be right and highly 'natural'. But persons of such intelligence and individuality aren't, when it comes to forming a confident mutual understanding, easily reassured in the face of

84

delicacies, unconsciousnesses, inhibitions and complexities that stand in the way. Birkin says something that both startles and pleases her, so that she is moved to ask a question.

But he was shy, and did not say any more. So the moment passed for this time. And gradually a feeling of sorrow came over her.
'My life is unfulfilled,' she said.
'Yes,' he answered briefly, not wanting to hear this.
'And I feel as if nobody could ever really love me,' she said.
But he did not answer.

This last brief sentence refers us back to something that comes earlier in the same chapter—something that accounts for its being called 'Moony'. Ursula and Birkin had encountered one another unexpectedly. Supposing him to be in the south of France convalescing after an illness, she set out one evening on a walk towards the mill (he had lodgings in the mill-house). 'She would,' we are told of her intention, 'just see the pond before she went home'. The bright moon troubled her, so, as she approached the pond from above, she swerved into the trees that hid the steep bank, and finally arrived at that. She stood there, looking at the smooth black water and the moon floating on it. Then she saw a shadowy figure, and realized that Birkin had come back. She could hear him talking disconnectedly to himself.

'You can't go away,' he was saying. 'There is no away. You only withdraw upon yourself.'

Then he started picking up stones and throwing them at the reflection of the moon, trying to obliterate it. But always the dancing dispersed fragments sought the old centre, till the moon was there again. He persisted, and Ursula could bear it no longer.

She slipped from her seat and went down to him, saying:
'You won't throw stones at it any more, will you?'
'How long have you been there?'
'All the time. You won't throw any more stones, will you?'
'I wanted to see if I could make it quite go off the pond,' he said.
'Yes, it was horrible, really. Why should you hate the moon? . . .'

Clearly, it is some vague, if profound, apprehension that makes her call the stoning of the reflected moon 'horrible'—a sense that the animus expressed in the directed stones is something she has herself to fear. That sense is well-founded; for the moon that Birkin tries to shatter is Western idealized love, and—inevitably, she having been bred in our civilization—Ursula, when she asks for love, means the love that could, and should, be 'perfect' and remain that till death. But not only does Birkin recoil from the implicit self-commitment to utter intimacy, and the other falsities and impossibilities; he knows that he must get Ursula to recognize for what it is the inherent matriarchal drive that, obstinately, innocent, takes cover in the feminine devotion to 'perfect love', an idealizing assumption identified with the love that is to be returned by the loved and loving man. Birkin has had experience of Hermione, and the immediate prelude to the stone-throwing is:

'Cybele—curse her! The accursed Syria Dea! Does one grudge it her? What else is there—?'

Birkin's colloquy with Ursula by the mill-pond ended happily, in spite of the fact that in her understanding she was dazed. But Birkin, the next day, thinking things over,

was frightened. He was tired too, when he had reached this length of speculation.

Behind the fear was the whole organic complex of Laurentian thought. Birkin (who in this, as in other things, *is* Lawrence) insisted on the subordination of love to individuality—on his horror of the notion of ideal love as the perfect intimacy that is merging (a horror in keeping with his diagnosis of Western civilization).

Was this then all that remained? Was there left now nothing but to break off from the happy creative being, was the time up? Is our day of creative life finished?

The relation between this fear and Birkin's insistence regarding love is that the creativity threatened by industrial civilization, with its power to mechanize what lives in it or by it, depends on the robustly individual being—the profoundly creative individuality that can draw on the source that lies deep down, uncontrolled by the ego, and is the source of spontaneity. For every significant artist can say, with Blake, of the creative works he produces: 'Though I call them mine, I know that they are not mine.'

I needn't offer to discuss 'the other way' of breaking off from 'the happy creative being', the way for which Birkin's symbol is the West African fetish he had seen at Halliday's (chapter VII, 'Totem'). What for Birkin (and Lawrence) is the primary concern is the contrasting way, the way that menaces *us*.

It would be done differently by the white races. The white races, having the arctic north behind them, the vast abstraction of ice and snow, would fulfil a mystery of ice-destructive knowledge, snow-abstract annihilation.

* * *

Birkin thought of Gerald. He was one of these white wonderful demons from the north, fulfilled in the destructive frost mystery. And was he fated to pass away in this knowledge, this one process of frost-knowledge, death by perfect cold? Was he a messenger, an omen of the universal dissolution into whiteness and snow?

I have contrived, by means of the quoting, just to touch on what, fairly treated, shades off into, or becomes, the cosmic element in Laurentian thought. It deserves attention that I won't try to give it now; it would be too large an excursus. And without that, the inevitability of Gerald's death in the snow of the high Tyrol will be felt as such by the reader of *Women in Love*— and 'inevitable' means that the significance will come convincingly through to him.

Birkin thinks commonly of Gerald as a friend, a human being to be affectionately concerned about. At the wedding-reception (chapter II, 'Shortlands') Mrs Crich has an odd conversation with Birkin which ends thus:

She looked round the room, vaguely. Birkin could not guess what she was looking for, nor what she was thinking. Evidently she noticed her sons.

'Are my children all there?' she asked him abruptly.

He laughed, startled, afraid perhaps.

'I scarcely know them except Gerald,' he replied.

'Gerald!' she exclaimed. 'He's the most wanting of them all. You'd never think it, to look at him now, would you?'

'No,' said Birkin.

The mother looked across at her eldest son, stared at him heavily for some time.

'Aye' she said, in an incomprehensible monosyllable that sounded profoundly cynical. Birkin felt afraid, as if he dared not realize. And Mrs Crick moved away, forgetting him. But she returned on her traces.

'I should like him to have a friend,' she said. 'He has never had a friend.'

This is the aspect of Gerald that complements his self-sufficiency —for Mrs Crich, where her eldest son is concerned, has a subtle mother's insight into complexities, undercurrents and contradictions. Birkin too is aware, in a different way, that Gerald needs a friend, the awareness not being separable from the recognition arrived at by Birkin in himself of the need he has of a permanent man-friend whom he can rely on absolutely. This permanency of a special kind of friendship goes, ideally, with the vowed permanency in marriage (as distinguished from 'love'), his belief in which he tries to explain to Ursula, who demands love. Only love, real love, can justify marriage, but, there being no such thing as 'perfect love', the essential marriage-understanding is that the relationship between the two individual beings shall be permanent, transcending change.

These that follow are his reflections by the mill-pond when, having fed his despair on the menace represented by Gerald, the white demon from the north (the significance of the phrase is brought out by pairing him, in contrast, with the West African fetish), he breaks off in recoil:

Suddenly his strange, strained attention gave way, he couldn't attend to these mysteries any more. There was another way, the way of freedom. There was the paradisal entry into pure, single being, the individual soul taking precedence over love and desire for union, stronger than any pangs of emotion, a lovely state of free proud singleness, which accepted the obligation of the permanent connection with others; and with *the* other, submits to the yoke and leash of love, but never forfeits its own proud individual singleness, even while it loves and yields.

The other thing that, in her uncannily spontaneous way, Mrs Crich says about Gerald is that 'He's the most wanting of them all,' meaning, it seems, by 'wanting' that he's both the most lacking in self-sufficiency, and the most apt to demand vital support from others. Well, we know, though it's not apparent outwardly, that he has a burden of dreadful memory: as a boy, he accidentally killed his brother. But what is clearly of major

importance in its bearing on our civilization is his pure instru-
mentality; I refer to the point that Gudrun makes when, confirming her sister's observation ('He's got *go*, anyhow'), she
remarks: 'The unfortunate thing is, where does his *go* go to . . .?'
Ursula has already said: 'He'll have to die soon, when he's made
every possible improvement, and there will be nothing more to
improve.' He lacks the creativity that comes from the source—
from the inlet through which the unknown, without access to
which there is no creation, enters. The ego is closed to that, and
will belongs to the ego; Gerald's strong will, therefore, is doomed
to automatism: it can't achieve spontaneity, the condition of
significance.

He discovers—or demonstrates—this last truth well before the
crisis that drives him, for rescue or refuge, to throw himself on
Gudrun.

The whole system was now so perfect that Gerald was hardly necessary any more.

It was so perfect that sometimes a strange fear came over him, and
he did not know what to do. He went on for some years in a sort of
trance of activity. What he was doing seemed supreme, he was almost
like a divinity. He was a pure and exalted activity.

But now he had succeeded—he had finally succeeded. And once or
twice lately, when he was alone in the evening and had nothing to do,
he had suddenly stood up in terror, not knowing what he was. And he
went to the mirror, and looked long and closely at his own face, at
his own eyes, seeking for something. He was afraid, in mortal dry
fear, but he knew not what of . . . He was afraid that one day he would
break down and be a purely meaningless babble lapping round a
darkness.

But his will yet held good. . . .

This is in chapter XVII, 'The Industrial Magnate'. The collapse
comes in chapter XXIV, which is called 'Death and Love'. The
death is the slow and very dreadful death of his father; love is
Gudrun. While the protracted battle not to die goes on, we are
told of Gerald: 'He threw away everything now—he only wanted
the relation established with her.' At last Thomas Crich dies, and
Gerald, of whom it can hardly be said that he loved or respected
his father, knows that the death, the annihilation, leaves a void
that is insufferable.

After dinner, faced with the ultimate experience of his own nothing-ness, he turned aside. He pulled on his boots, put on his coat, and set out to walk in the night.

He goes, having stopped in the churchyard at his father's grave for a moment, to the Brangwen family house in Beldover. The front-door being not yet secured, he enters, and, in his clay-heavy boots, climbs the stairs and finds Gudrun's bedroom. We have been told at the end of chapter XVII, when Gerald is still the calculating master of his actions: 'He had found his most satis-factory relief in women.' Gudrun certainly knew that, and it is for relief that he goes to her now. Of course, they attract one another, and their relation comes—but unpromisingly—under the head of 'love'. In the penultimate chapter, 'Snowed Up', when they know that they hate one another murderously, Gud-run tells him that, on this occasion at Beldover, it was for pity, not love, that she hadn't turned him away.

There is no need to trace the graph of changing tension between them from the clandestine night in the Brangwen home to the moment when Birkin, with Ursula, who can't bear the snow-world, departs for Verona. When Birkin and Ursula are gone, the hatred and contempt that are now the reality of what passed for love between the other pair become rapidly overt. Gerald wants to kill Gudrun, and she knows it; but she cultivates close relations with Loerke, whom Gerald treats with intensely hostile contempt. With nothing left but energy, physical skill and auto-matism, he skis all day and into the gathering night, till he lapses out in utter exhaustion; his 'go' goes into the cold and snow that are for him the world.

Birkin, telegraphed for, hurries back with Ursula from Verona. At the sight of the frozen corpse—and the face, he is badly stricken: 'Cold, mute, material!' He remembers

how once Gerald had clutched his hand, with a warm, momentaneous grip of final love. For one second—then let go again, let go for ever. If he had kept true to that clasp, death would not have mattered. Those who die, and dying still can love, still believe, do not die. They live still in the beloved. Gerald might still have been living in the spirit with Birkin, even after death.

The Gerald who had become the man friend with whom Birkin could have had the 'eternal union' would have been a

Gerald who learnt to know in what, for him, life 'centred'. We may perhaps believe, with Birkin, that Gerald might, with better luck—might, if Gudrun had been other—have learnt it, having become another man; but he didn't. And that lack was the basic deficiency in him that Gudrun recoiled from, though—with no man but Gerald to bring it home to her—she never fully knew it, and could never have consented to entertain a full knowledge.

All life, all life resolved itself into this: tick-tack, tick-tack, tick-tack; then the striking of the hour ... Gerald could not save her from it. He, his body, his motion, his life, it was the same ticking, the same twitching across the dial, a horrible mechanical twitching forward over the face of the hours. What were his kisses, his embraces? She could hear their tick-tack, tick-tack.

*   *   *

Oh God, when I think of Gerald, and his work—those offices at Beldover, and the mines—it makes my heart sick. What *have* I to do with it—and him thinking he can be a lover to a woman! One might as well ask it of a self-satisfied lamp-post. The men with their eternal jobs—and their eternal mills of God that keep on grinding at nothing! It is too boring, just boring. How did I come to take him seriously at all!

Ursula, on the other hand, so different from Gudrun, knew that she had for husband a man whose individual life was open to the deep source, to the unknown, and who had his part in the creativity that kept civilization rooted and changing—that is alive. But he couldn't have been that without her.

IV

'THE CAPTAIN'S DOLL'

'NOTHING is important but life': my acceptance of this Laurentian dictum as laying an essential emphasis for any account of Lawrence's own importance has won me a good deal of adverse comment. For instance, a well-known indefatigable publicist on the themes of pornography has recently adduced—and endorsed—a philosopher's criticism of myself as one who, in my characterization of Lawrence's genius, makes great use of the word 'life', but seems quite unaware of the need to attempt some distinguishing between the diverse values it covers. Since the philosopher has a post in a university English department and is articulate and confident, I had remarked that, his assumption being that the distinctions would have to be defined philosophically, he must have done, educationally, a good deal of damage. But even when they have not earned also a standing as philosophers, can we trust lecturers in 'English' to point out—or to know—that the most important kind of thought is decidedly *not* philosophical?

It is significant that a representative of Oxford 'English' who enjoys a reputation as a critic chose to exemplify (I suppose) the way in which I am exposed to adverse comment in relation to a perversely imputed criterion by assuming that I think highly (I do) of 'The Daughters of the Vicar', Lawrence's very obviously relevant tale. The theme entails the beautiful, proud and good Miss Mary's being pressed by desperate poverty and the family's expectation into marrying the curate, Mr Massy, who is even unaware that everyone recoils from him as, in his 'inhuman being', a kind of abortion (but he is rich).

'He seems to me nearly an imbecile,' said Miss Louisa. Miss Mary, quiet and beautiful, was silent for a moment.
'Oh, no,' she said. 'Not imbecile—'
'Well then—he reminds me of a six months' child—or a five months' child—as if he didn't have time to get developed enough before he was born.'

My Oxford critic pointed out that Mr Massy, who has (besides
money) self-confidence and a strong will, is unmistakably alive,
and must therefore share in any importance one imputed to life;
so that the appraisal of Lawrence in which my endorsement of
Lawrence's dictum counts for so much must be dismissed as
fallacious.

Miss Mary's inner state is evoked for us here:

'Yes,' said Miss Mary, slowly. 'There is something lacking. But there
is something wonderful in him: and he is really *good*—'
'Yes,' said Miss Louisa, 'it doesn't seem right that he should be.
What right has *that* to be called goodness!'
'But it *is* goodness,' persisted Mary. Then she added, with a laugh:
'And come, you wouldn't deny that as well.'
There was a doggedness in her voice. She went about very quietly.
In her soul, she knew what was going to happen. She knew that Mr
Massy was stronger than she, and that she must submit to what he was.
Her physical self was prouder, stronger than he, her physical self
disliked and despised him. But she was in the grip of his moral, mental
being. And she felt the days allotted out to her. And her family
watched.

I don't suggest that such a critic as my Oxford one necessarily
dismisses Lawrence's tale as undistinguished, but I insist that he
shows himself incapable of a critical (that is, a full) appreciation
of it—or of the essential Laurentian genius. That genius is so
important to our civilization, so necessary for the correcting of
its fatal incapacity, that everyone who really cares sees that a
duly articulate appreciation is indispensable, and that the minority
capable of such needs to be as large as it can be made. 'Art-speech
is the only speech': that is Lawrence's way of making the
point I make when I say that our civilization desperately
lacks the thought it has lost the power even to recognize *as*
thought—the thought that entails the creative writer's kind of
creativity.

But in arriving, after the start I have made, here—at this re-
emphasized recognition—I, as the insistent expositor, find myself,
the recognition being so fundamental, faced with a problem of
expository method. I have said that the most important words are
more than ambiguous in a way that defies dictionary definition.

The word before us now is 'life'. I had thought of inquiring, in an examination of 'The Daughters of the Vicar', into the characteristics, the creative ways, that together make my Oxford critic's objection manifestly absurd, and then proceeding to deal with a series of progressively subtler instances or cases in Lawrence's work. But the live, the *living* nature itself of Lawrence's thought soon brought out its unamenableness to orderly exposition of that kind. One might say that the complex totality of *Women in Love* is needed to convey the superlative force and nuance, the supreme value, the word 'life' has for his comprehensive creative thought.

Nevertheless, something less comprehensive than his greatest novel is required for the expositor's purposes—which (let me insist) conceive their success as being identical with supersession by the Laurentian 'art-speech'. I have then decided to proceed by considering one of the finest of Lawrence's tales, 'The Captain's Doll'. The theme of that is love—the relations between Captain Hepburn and Hannele, to the treatment of which the history of the Captain's relations with his wife is ancillary.

The same theme of course, love—the relations between men and women coming under that head, plays a major and inseparable part in Lawrence's supreme inquiry into life, *Women in Love*. But the relations between Hepburn and Hannele have nothing corresponding to the comprehensive context that makes *Women in Love* the great Laurentian inquest into our civilization and what menaces it—the drive that impels it to self-destruction. The limitation, the very much less intricate complexity, lends itself to the expository treatment of Lawrence's basic thought; for the treatment of the love-theme in 'The Captain's Doll' is equally a treatment of the life-theme—bears, that is, directly on the philosopher's and the critic's objections to the indeterminateness of the word 'life'.

I think that my reader will do well to read along with 'The Captain's Doll' an expository essay of Lawrence's own: '. . . Love was once a Little Boy' (*Reflections on the Death of a Porcupine* in which it appeared is included in *Phoenix II*). It serves to emphasize the fact that the tale is amply enough invested with a complexity of its own, and is full of very relevant felicities. It is enough at the moment to quote one of them:

Hate is not the opposite of love. The real opposite of love is individuality. We live in the age of individuality, we call ourselves the servants of love. That is to say, we enact a perpetual paradox.

We have here what might be said to be a general statement of the problem that faces the Captain and Hannele in 'The Captain's Doll'. The evoking of the problem as, in its formidable changing concreteness, it enacts itself between them (each, of course, feeling it in his or her own distinctive way) is marvellously done, the doing depending largely on Lawrence's genius for dramatic dialogue.

Of the pair of principal actors it is the Captain mainly who changes for us. In the opening he is impressive; our sense of him is the sense generated for us by the two women—Hannele (the Countess Johanna zu Rassentlow) and Mitchka (the Baroness von Prielau-Carolath) who has visited her friend as she sits in the captain's attic putting the finishing touches to her portrait-doll of him. That Hannele, like her friend, is an aristocrat has obviously its significance for us. The doll itself registers her sense of his impressiveness—though an observation of the captain's towards the end clinches our growing conviction that it registers something else in her too. Mitchka, who pays her brief visit in his absence, is uneasy lest, returning, he should find her there. She hears steps on the stone stairs, and slips hastily out to look. It is a false alarm; she comes back with Martin, a German officer-friend.

Of Hannele we are told:

She was a fair woman with dark-blond hair and a beautiful fine skin. Her face seemed luminous, a certain quick gleam of life about it as she looked up at the man.

The 'quick gleam of life' is the index of what makes her important to the captain. His mysteriously impressive distinction is what the Baroness now has the opportunity to insist on in a natural way.

Mitchka was wandering round the room, looking at everything, and saying: 'Beautiful! But beautiful! Such good taste! A man, and such good taste. No, they don't need a woman. No, look here, Martin, the Captain Hepburn has arranged all this room himself. Here you have the man. Do you see? So simple, yet so elegant. He needs no woman.'

THOUGHT, WORDS AND CREATIVITY

Seeing 'various astronomical apparatus' lying upon the table, she goes on:

'And he reads the stars. Only think—he is an astronomer and reads the stars. Queer, queer, people, the English!'
'He is Scottish,' said Hannele.

The visitors depart, and when, after a brief while, during which Hannele betrays her uneasy sense that she hasn't, in respect of him, arrived at anything approaching a finality of summing-up, he comes in, he impresses us as a man of whom the very quality that explains such uneasiness at the same time explains why she should be drawn to him. His idiosyncrasy of speech is, in tone and attitude, often surprising, but the unexpectedness doesn't give the effect of being casual, cranky or evasive. 'He had,' we are told, 'an odd way of answering, as if he were only half attending, as if he were thinking of something else.' But actually the 'as if' is deceptive; the air of 'only half attending' comes of a habit of profoundly felt responsibility in the Laurentian sense of the word. Hannele's inarticulate intuition of the nature of the masculine strength in him is at the centre of her impressed response to the poise in which it shows itself; but the inevitable implicitness of the intuition goes with uneasiness: necessarily she gets surprises that move her to unadmiring wonder and indignant anger. The immediate occasion concerns his wife, and her having got wind of his liaison with the German aristocrat. He answers Hannele about his lateness:

'Well, as a matter of fact, I was talking with the Colonel.'
'About me?'
'Yes. It was about you.'
She went pale as she sat looking up into his face. But it was impossible to tell whether there was distress on his dark brow or not.
'Anything nasty?' she said.
'Well, yes. It was rather nasty. Not about you, I mean. But rather awkward for me.'

His whole—at any rate, it seems so—idiosyncratic habit of being is made potently present to us in his speech, though, when we look carefully at a passage of the marvellously done *tête-à-tête*, we see that the effect of a characteristic positiveness that attends, paradoxically, on the 'straying voice' owes a great deal to the distinctive presence that the artist, Hannele, has rendered in the doll, which, though we haven't in brute fact seen it, we do see, and have throughout the tale before our eyes.

'She watched him. But still he said no more.
'What was it?' she said.
'Oh, well—only what I expected. They seem to know rather too much about you—about you and me, I mean. Not that anybody cares one bit, unofficially. The trouble is, they are probably going to have to take official notice.'
'Why?'
'Oh, well—it appears that my wife has been writing letters to the Major-General. He is one of her family acquaintances—known her all his life. And I suppose she's been hearing rumours. In fact I know she has. She said so in her letter to me.'
'And what do you say to her then?'
'Oh, I tell her I'm all right—not to worry.'
'You don't expect *that* to stop her worrying, do you?' she asked.
'Oh, I don't know. Why should she worry?' he said.
'I think she might have some reason,' said Hannele. 'You've not seen her for a year. And if she adores you—'
'Oh, I don't think she adores me. I think she quite likes me.'
'Do you think you matter as little as that to her?'
'I don't see why not. Of course, she likes to feel safe about me.'
'But now she doesn't feel safe?'
'No—exactly. Exactly. That's the point. That's where it is. The Colonel advises me to go home on leave.'
He sat gazing with curious bright, dark, unseeing eyes at the doll which he held by one arm. It was an extraordinary likeness of himself, true even to the smooth parting of his hair, and his peculiar way of fixing his dark eyes.

It is plain, then, that, in the evocation of his impressive individuality, the visual element (which is so much more than merely visual) plays an essential part—one inseparable from his idiosyncratic mode of speech. The phrase, 'fixing his dark eyes', is one of a diversity of ways that, taken together, establish firmly the significant paradox: the 'straying voice' is a manifestation of a peculiar kind of strength. 'Dark' here carries the suggestion it brings from its Laurentian use in potent contexts—a suggestion antipathetic, the nature of thought being the theme, to the ethos of *la clarté* and 'clear and distinct ideas'.

THOUGHT, WORDS AND CREATIVITY

I recall places in *The Plumed Serpent* which, discussing that book, I have already pointed to,[1] and notably the colloquy between Kate and Ramón in the opening pages of the fourth chapter. Both of them express disgust with the ego and its will, she being in a hesitant mood in which she recoils from the hateful fascination of Mexico, but finds that she can't easily decide to return to the old familiar Europe. The following passage comes a little further on in the same chapter (page 84):

> But the dark-faced natives, with their strange soft flame of life wheeling upon a dark void: were they centreless and widdershins too, as so many white men now are? The strange, soft flame of courage in the black Mexican eyes. But still it was not knit to a centre, that centre which is the soul of a man in a man.

Ramón has already intimated to Kate what difference a 'centre' makes—that is, repudiating mere will, told her what a 'centre' is and must be.

'And what do you find?'
'My own manhood.'

'Manhood', the word Ramón uses, is responsibility—the profound, the ultimate human responsibility defined by Conrad's art in *The Secret Sharer*. Ramón says of it:

> '. . . It comes from—from the middle—from the God. Beyond me, at the middle, is the God. And the God gives me my manhood, then leaves me to it.'

That is, the ultimate responsibility is of its nature essentially human; it is the distinctive characteristic of the human status, though the demonstrative realization of this truth is so much the reverse of usual. We recall Blake's distinction between the 'ego' and the 'identity'. The 'ego' is the enclosed ego—enclosed against the well-head, through which life and creativity bubble up from the unknown. The young ship's-captain's manhood tells him that no code, no chart, no moral system will solve the problem of responsibility that confronts him, and both Kate and Ramón are conscious that they desperately need the peace, the exacting satisfaction of disinterestedness. But life that speaks from the well-head must still speak as the individual 'I'; there is for the living no

---

[1] See p. 52 ff. above.

presence of life but in individuality, and human individuality at its most individual is Blakean 'identity'—life that is at its maximum,[1] most itself, most alive. Lawrence, covering with the one word 'ego' what the Blakean terms together offer to do, is implicitly recognizing the continuity within the individual being of 'identity' with 'ego' that makes the discovery of one's 'manhood' a paradoxical achievement and the irreplaceable responsibility of the individual a matter of being 'left to it' by 'the God'.

The Captain's profound idiosyncrasy, then, that goes with the straying voice isn't such as to make Hannele feel 'safe' in regard to their mutual relations, though she responds to his distinction, and it is a sense of something in the mystery of him that draws her to him and continues to do so. Having been told of the Colonel's advice, she asked 'And will you go?'

'I don't know. I don't know.' His head remained bent, he seemed to muse rather vaguely. 'I don't know,' he repeated. 'I can't make up my mind what I shall do.'

His 'I can't make up my mind' is not an avowal of weak irresolution; nor, in what follows, does he merely waver, but moves, considering perceived complexities, towards a decided, but delicate intimation of a resulting positive attitude.

'Would you like to go?' she asked.
He lifted his brows and looked at her. Her heart always melted in her when he looked straight at her with his black eyes, and that curious, bright unseeing look that was more like second sight than direct human vision. She never knew what he saw when he looked at her. 'No,' he said quite simply. 'I don't *want* to go. I don't think I've any desire at all to go to England.'
'Why not?' she asked.
'I can't say.' Then again he looked at her, and a curious white light seemed to shine on his eyes, as he smiled slowly with his mouth, and said:
'I suppose you ought to know if anybody does.'
A glad, half-frightened look came on her face.
'You mean you don't want to leave me?' she asked, breathless.
'Yes. I suppose that's what I mean.'
'But you aren't sure?'

[1] cf. 'At the maximum of our imagination we are religious.'

99

'Yes, I am, I'm quite sure,' he said, and the curious smile lingered on his face, and the strange light shone in his eyes.

'That you don't want to leave me?' she stammered, looking aside.

'Yes, I'm quite sure I don't want to leave you,' he repeated. He had a curious, very melodious Scottish voice. But it was the incomprehensible smile on his face that convinced and frightened her.

Yet the Captain's sureness, though it gives Hannele pleasure, doesn't make her feel safe, and, actually, she isn't safe: the development of the tale shows chance playing a crucial part. And Hannele's feelings are mixed:

it was all like a mystery to her, as if one of the men from Mars were loving her. And she was heavy and spell-bound, and she loved the spell that bound her. But also she didn't love it.

She is exasperated with him even to the point of hating him, because he seems determined not to think about the future, but to treat the unforeseeableness of chance as an excuse for refusing to be responsible.

'What *is* of any significance?' she insisted. She almost hated him.

'What is of any significance? Well, nothing to me, outside this room, at this minute. Nothing in time or space matters to me.'

'Yes, *this minute*!' she repeated bitterly. 'But then there's the future. I've got to live in the future.'

'The future! The future! The future is used up every day. The future to me is like a big tangle of black thread. Every morning you begin to untangle one loose end—and that's your day. And every evening you break off and throw away what you've untangled, and the heap is so much less: just one thread less, one day less. That's all the future matters to me.'

The Captain, in response to her non-acceptance of his soothing assurances, says more in the same idiosyncratic and spontaneous way—and the reader, at least, commits himself or herself to hazarding that, whatever the explanation lying ahead may turn out to be, it won't be the mere limpness of irresponsibility. But the 'mystery' for Hannele can hardly be reassuring. 'Words', Hepburn tells her, 'mean so little. They mean nothing. And all that one thinks and plans doesn't amount to anything. Let me feel that we are together, and I don't care about all the rest.'

The almost immediate arrival of the wife in person is a disconcerting surprise—not primarily (at any rate for the reader) because of its suddenness, but because of the shocking improbability of so vulgarly null and complete a feminine egoist as a wife for the original of the portrait-doll. The improbability affects Hannele by precipitating a shift from awe to the other extreme of the range of varying attitudes that correspond to her very unstable sense of the reality implicit in the mystery, the 'straying' unruffleable inexplicitness of the Captain. Already, on the day of the wife's visit to the studio, joint 'shop' of Mitchka and Hannele (who hasn't even a faint suspicion that the visitor is the Captain's actual wife), we have been told:

That evening Hannele was restless ... most uneasy because she seemed to have forgotten him in the three days whilst he had been away. He seemed to have quite disappeared out of her. She could hardly even remember him. He had become so insignificant to her she was dazed.

Now she wanted to see him again, to know if it was really so. She felt that he was coming. She felt that he was already putting out some influence towards her. But what? And was he real? Why had she made his doll? And why had his doll been so important, if he was nothing? Why had she shown it to that funny little woman this afternoon? ... Martin was real; German men were real to her. But this other, he was simply not there. ... Now he was absent, she couldn't even *imagine* him. He had gone out of her imagination, and even when she looked at his doll she saw nothing but a barren puppet.

But when, going out on to the landing between her attic and his to listen for him, she hears him talking to someone as they come up, she at once confirms her 'lurking suspicion' that there might be 'something else':

And instantly she heard his voice she was afraid again. She knew there *was* something there.

* * *

This is what she had to reckon with, this recoil from the one to the other. When he was present, he seemed so terribly real. When he was absent he was completely vague, and her men of her own race seemed so absolutely the only reality.

Here we have the theme of the tale; the problem to which the answer, the complex answer, is arrived at by shared ordeal, or lived experience gone through between Hannele and the Captain.

Chance plays its part—as, very promptly, in the death of 'the little woman' by a fall from the third floor of the hotel on to the pavement below. She was necessary to the significance of the tale—necessary to the development in Hannele of a difficult enlightenment about the Captain's 'mysteriousness', a development which entails, inescapably, a new insight into herself and the nature of love. The immediate outcome of Mrs Hepburn's advent is to intensify to an extreme the incomprehensibility of the Captain to Hannele. The Captain remains what he was, but Hannele is baffled into an angrily incredulous blankness in which her power of believing in her love loses itself.

The *tête-à-tête* between her on the landing between the attics and him on his stool outside the window, on the roof with his telescope, is done with Laurentian genius. He tells her that his wife has come, and that he is going to join her in the Vier Jahreszeiten. He had no idea of the blank amazement in which Hannele listened to this.

'But—' she stammered. 'But doesn't she expect you to make *love* to her?'

'Oh, yes, she expects that. You bet she does: womanlike.'

'And you?—the question had a dangerous ring.

'Why, I don't mind, really, you know, if it's only for a short time. I'm used to her. I've always been fond of her, you know—and so if it gives her any pleasure—why, I like her to get what pleasure out of life she can.'

'But *you*—you yourself! Don't *you* feel anything?' Hannele's amazement was reaching the point of incredulity. She began to feel that he was making it up. It was all so different from her own point of view. To sit there so quiet and make such statements in all good faith: no, it was impossible.

'I don't consider I count,' he said naïvely.

We don't wonder that to Hannele it seems all so ridiculous that she could die, she says, with laughter. But actually such seeming, even at moments of her completest and angriest alienation, doesn't represent every element in her responsive attitude. In fact, the farcical comedy of the *tête-à-tête* isn't really farcical comedy to her—or to us; the scene has a context, and what of this has gone before makes us sensitive to the idiosyncrasy of the Captain's answers, which are unforeseeable and distinguished, and of which we are sure that they *mean* something—something basically important—to him, and that we shall in due course appreciate the meaning. We are given ample reason for being aware that he speaks out of a poised, profound and delicate equanimity.

'But do you *never* count then?' she asked, and there was a touch of derision, of laughter in her tone. He took no offence.

It is characteristic of him to take no offence where almost anyone else in his place would show signs of a ruffled ego.

'Well—very rarely,' he said. 'I count very little. That's how life appears to me. One matters so *very* little.'
She felt dizzy with astonishment. And he called himself a man!

The exasperation that makes itself felt in that last brief sentence is very close to resentment; she herself does take offence: this is an essential datum in the situation, necessary to the convincing finality of the end—that is, to the significance of the whole creative demonstration.

'But if you matter so very little, what do you do anything at all for?' she asked.
'Oh, one has to. And then, why not? Why not do things even if oneself hardly matters. Look at the moon. It doesn't matter in the least to the moon whether I exist or whether I don't. So why should it matter to me?'

One would hardly say that she understands this; but it isn't for her either the confident logic of madness or mere willed flippancy. The tone of her part in the sustained dialogue seems to establish that.

There was a long and pregnant silence: we should not like to say pregnant with what.
'And so I don't mean anything to you at all?' she said.
'I didn't say that,' he replied.
'Nothing means anything to you,' she challenged.
'I don't say that.'
'Whether it's your wife—or me—or the moon—*toute la même chose.*'
'No—no—that's hardly the way to look at it.'

These one recognizes as serious answers, not mere evasive irresponsibilities, though one wouldn't say that Hannele at the time was capable of finding them satisfying or intelligible. The truth clearly is that the assumptions in her, the premises, ungrantable by him, were for her so firmly established, so invincibly axiomatic, that there was no language common to them in which he could make his position intelligible to her. It has to be added too that he hadn't yet arrived at a firm grasp of any total positive judgment formed by his 'manhood' as the upshot of experience. There was complexity and there was what might look like self-contradiction, and no clean line between them. The essential problem that, once his wife is dead, will face the Captain is a variant of that which faced Birkin when, watched from cover by the unseen Ursula, he tried to shatter out of existence with stones the reflection of the moon on the mill-pond.

In the immediately ensuing scene we learn something about the complication that makes a major difference between the Captain and Birkin. It is not merely that the Captain has a wife instead of the past represented by Hermione Roddice, but that this wife is so classily vulgar and assured, so *borné*, cliché-conventional and pettily ego-bound, that no intelligent man would find her possible to live with, and at the same time Captain Hepburn (who doesn't want to retire from the army) has an intense solicitude for her happiness. Lawrence doesn't *tell* us all this; it is conveyed to us in the manner and substance of her talk (to be confirmed later by the Captain). She runs across Hannele in the Domplatz, and sweeps her off to tea in the Vier Jahreszeiten, the hotel where she is now staying with her husband—whom she assumes to be the victim, not of Hannele's attractions, but of the dark Baronin's. The doing, the way in which her invulnerability is brought out, is a triumph of Lawrence's dramatic genius.

An unshakably female and absolutist ego conditions the speech-facility she enjoys—which runs essentially to cliché. Her aim being to ensure that the Baronin shall be aware of the certain frustration awaiting her seductive charm, the little lady is intent on impressing to that end the assumed mere loyal friend of the dangerous beauty. She sends her readily obliging husband off on some errand or other, and settles down to an unhampered tactical chatter. In it, all unawares, she exposes herself thoroughly for the petty banality of a woman she is. 'It has been his one aim in life to make my life happy.' But she has already said: 'We poor women! We are a

guilty race, I am afraid.' She is seeking to impress on the listener
(for that is Hannele's role in the talk) that, while she approves of
her husband's having that 'one aim', regarding herself, she is not
excessively puritanical or self-constrictively proper.

'I fear I am rather old-fashioned. But never mind. I can see the
attractions in other men—can't I indeed! There was a perfectly exqui-
site creature—he was a very clever engineer—but much, much more
than *that*. But never mind.' The little heroine sniffed as if there were
perfume in the air, folded her jewelled hands, and resumed: 'However—
I know what it is myself to flutter round the flame. You know I'm
Irish myself, and we Irish can't help it. Oh, I wouldn't be English for
anything. Just that little touch of imagination, you know. . . .' The
little laugh tinkled. 'And that's what makes me able to sympathize
with my husband even when, perhaps, I shouldn't.'

Actually, in any meaningful sense of the word she has *no*
imagination: an extreme deficiency of imagination conditions
the confidently articulate stupidity she is gifted with. And she is
incapable of sympathizing with her husband, who as an imaginable independent male life doesn't exist for her:

'I don't think he ever thought of another woman as being flesh and
blood, after he knew me.'

That, for any reader of the tale, ridiculous though it is, is a revealing judgment. As for his wanting to stay on in the army, his wife's
comment on that is: 'I have never known him before go against
my real wishes.'

The effect on Hannele of 'the little woman's' calculated feminine talk is catastrophic:

Ach! Ach! Hannele wrung her hands to think of *herself* being mixed
up with him. And he had seemed to her so manly. He seemed to have
so much male passion in him. And yet—the little lady! 'My husband
has *always* been *perfectly sweet* to me.'
Think of it! On his knees too. And his 'Yes, dear! Certainly.
Certainly.' Not that he was afraid of the little lady. He was just committed to her, as he might have been committed to gaol, or committed to paradise. Had she been dreaming, to be in love with him?
Oh, oh, she wished so much she had never been.

This insistence is essentially relevant to Lawrence's thought. In
one important sense of 'love', she loves him still; there is a strong

and lasting attraction. She recognizes this in a virtually simultaneous way.

So much for charm. She had better have stuck to her own sort of men, Martin, for instance, who was a gentleman and a daring soldier, and a queer soul and pleasant to talk to. Only he hadn't any *magic*. Magic? The very word made her writhe. Magic? Swindle. Swindle, that was all it amounted to. Magic!

And yet—let us not be too hasty. If the magic had *really* been there, on those evenings in that great lofty attic. Had it? Yes, she was bound to admit it.

★   ★   ★

You could call it an illusion if you liked. But an illusion which is a real experience is worth having. Perhaps this disillusion was a greater illusion than the illusion itself. Perhaps all this disillusion of the little lady and the husband of the little lady was falser than the illusion and magic of those few evenings. Perhaps the long disillusion of life was falser than the brief moments of real illusion ... Only let the spell be upon her. It was all she longed for. And the thing she had to fight was the vulgarity of disillusion. The vulgarity of the little lady, the vulgarity of the husband of the little lady, the vulgarity of his insincerity, his 'Yes, dear. Certainly! Certainly!'—this was what she had to fight. He *was* vulgar and horrible, then. But also, the queer figure that sat alone on the roof watching the stars! The wonderful red flower of the cactus. The mystery that advanced with him as he came across the room after changing his tunic. The glamour and sadness of him, his silence, as he stooped unfastening his boots.

It is obvious that the little lady has no sense of any mystery in her husband; his *raison d'être* is to love her and make her life happy, and he doesn't dispute it. But he resists the pressure to resign his commission.

'But it *is* better for a man to be independent,' said Hannele.

'I know it is ... But it is also better for him to be *at home*. And I could get him a post in one of the observatories. He could do something in meteorological work.'

Hannele refused to answer any more.

She refuses because her sense of the Captain is outraged by the little lady's attitude to him. Hannele's love, in its lasting aspect, goes with a peculiar kind of awed respect—a respect inseparable from her reaction to the 'mystery' that it needs his presence or his voice to make her feel; the doll, admirable work of art as it is, doesn't in his absence do that—as she has found. The mystery can't be defined; neither can it be rendered in the most life-like doll, for the most life-like doll is not alive. The Captain's mystery is so potent because the life in him flows with unusual freedom from the source or well-head, so that he has the responsibility of one who is exquisitely sensitive to the unknown, and, being in delicate touch with the dark pregnancy, is capable of wonder— and of growth; that is, new livingness, which issues from the as yet unknown. When Hannele is informed by his presence she feels herself alive to the cosmos and to the wonderful red flower of the cactus.

Hannele, then, is very different from the Captain's wife, and the difference points to the part played by the latter in the total significance of the tale. But utter difference isn't all: there is something in their attitude towards marriage and the man that may be said to bracket them. Lawrence supplies intimations enough of what it is; this is representative:

Hannele had never been married, but she had come quite near enough to the realization of the event to know that such a scene *was* practically inevitable. An indispensable part of any honeymoon. Him on his knees with his heels up!

A hint that alerts us most pointedly is the double question that Hannele asks herself: why had she made that doll, and why had she shown it to the little lady? The implicit answer to the second is: that 'it's a counter-vaunt'. The total answer comes explicitly (but not from Hannele) near the end of the tale. She, as she couldn't have done earlier, implicitly accepts it at the very end. Her power of acceptance, the unstated (but not unevoked) changing inner condition that makes this possible, has been generated during the climb up to the glacier and the journey back. There is a change in both Hannele and the Captain. The mere fact that he had a wife had not told against the liaison. The problems that disturb Hannele are that the wife has revealed herself as the little lady and that he comports himself towards her as he does. How did he come to marry such a woman? And what significance are we to see in his treating her with such ignominious deference?

The catastrophe that promptly disposes of her enables him to give his own answer to this last question.

The very next day the Captain came back to his attic. Hannele did not know, until quite late at night when he tapped on her door. She knew his soft tap immediately.

'Won't you come over for a chat?' he said.

Though surprised, she comes over. He shows no such signs of self-consciousness as she had observed when they were present together at tea in the Vier Jahreszeiten, before his wife sent him off on her errand. Nor does he show signs of shock, though there is no doubt about the severe shock he suffered when he looked out of the window and saw her body on the pavement below.

Hannele was not listening to his words, but to his voice. . . . There was something a little automatic in what he said. But then that is always so when people have had a shock.

'It must have been terrible for you too,' she said.

'Ah, yes. At the time it was awful. Awful. I felt the smash right inside me, you know.'

'Awful!' she repeated.

'But now,' he said, 'I feel strangely happy about it. I feel happy about it. I feel happy for her sake, if you can understand that. I feel she has got out of some great tension. I feel she is free now for the first time in her life.'

We have, if we can, to take the Captain's word for the 'tension', since we can't associate anything that 'tension' suggests with the little lady Lawrence has evoked for us. And we can't wonder that Hannele sits 'in blank amazement' when the Captain gives the account of her that begins:

She was a gentle soul, and an original soul, but she was like a fairy who is condemned to live in houses and sit on furniture and all that, don't you know. It was never her nature.

We note that he doesn't resent the suggestion that these imaginings are incredible, so implicit is his faith in the matter-of-fact realness of what he says.

'But,' said Hannele, with a touch of mockery, 'how do you know you haven't made it all up—just to console yourself.'

'Oh, I've thought it long ago,' he said.

'Still,' she blurted, 'you may have invented it all—as a sort of consolation for—for—for your life.'

'Yes, I may,' he said. 'But I don't think so. It was her eyes. Did you never notice her eyes?'

From our very decided impression of her, it seems highly improbable that if we (and Hannele) *had* noticed her eyes, even paying special attention to them, they would have seemed to us to confirm the judgment in support of which he invokes them. What we do notice is that, in a quiet, almost unconscious way, he endorses Hannele's hesitantly expressed assumption that he has stood in need of being consoled while his wife was alive. That endorsement becomes a basic statement in the clearing-up between Hannele and himself that forms the end of the *nouvelle*:

'Then my wife: and that was my most terrible mistake. And I began the mistake of loving you.'

What is in question is the diversity of meanings covered by the word 'love', and more especially (for adverse judgment) the romantic conception of 'falling in love', with the attendant assumption that 'perfect love' is possible, and permanence likely to ensue. We recall that when Hannele learnt from the Captain that the little lady was his wife, she was astonished.

She had thought it might be an acquaintance—perhaps his aunt—or even an elder sister. 'But she's years older than you,' she added.

'Eight years,' he said. 'I'm forty-one.'

When he married he will have been in his twenty-second or -third year—not appreciably older; a good age for falling passionately in love, and believing that permanent happiness is possible—at any rate for oneself and one's beloved. It seems likely that the 'faery soul' hypothesis began as a part of the falling in love. At all events, the shock of his wife's death-fall, and the awakening and disturbing consequences of this in his intimate inner life, was that 'he was left with the bleeding ends of all his human relationships'. 'But then one never can know the whys and wherefores of one's passional changes.' He naturally had duties that called him to England; but he neither wrote to Hannele, nor wanted to think

of her. The winter passed, and there was a change, which is registered in this changed formulation: 'He could not even think of
Hannele.' But further: 'Anybody else he felt he need not think
about. He was deeply, profoundly thankful that his wife was dead.
It was an end of pity now. . . .'

Finally he went back to Germany to look for Hannele, from
whom he had got no answer to the letter he ultimately wrote.
He traced her at last to a small summer-resort in the Austrian
Tyrol, having discovered from a newspaper that she was rum-
oured to be engaged to the Herr Regierungsrat of the district, a
distinguished Austrian of fifty.

Hannele felt she would like to marry him . . . She would like him to
make her feel a queen in exile. No one had ever *quite* kissed her hand
as he had kissed it: with that sudden stillness, and strange, chivalric
abandon of himself. How he would abandon himself to her! —terribly
—wonderfully—perhaps a little horribly. His wife, whom he had
married late, had died after seven years of marriage. Hannele could
understand that too. One or the other must die.

She became engaged. But something made her hesitate before
marriage.

The Captain encountered them walking together; when she
recognized him 'she went pale'. The promptness with which,
after, invited by her at that first meeting, he had come to tea at
the place where she was staying, they arranged to make an excursion together to the glacier at the valley's head suggests that
the something which had made her hesitate before marrying the
Herr Regierungsrat was a sense of a vital relationship that she
found to be a crucial fact in her life.

Their making the excursion together was an implicit recognition of a need to clear up their relations with one another in the
hope of coming to terms. The fact that (to quote a phrase that I
have quoted before in this book) they 'were not in good company
together' doesn't make the joint expedition at the same time any
the less an implicit recognition that they were very strongly drawn
to one another. Actually, mutual irritation gives a distinctive tone
to their companionship; they were conscious of differences that
no doubt insisted on being canvassed, and the changing effort and
circumstances of the ascent helped.

The Captain was able to bring up the question of the doll with seeming casualness. They were in the last of the valleys before the glacier, and sat down by one of the streams to eat some lunch. 'The water poured with all the greed and lust of unloosed water over the stones':

As Alexander was putting the bread back into his shoulder-sack, he exclaimed: 'Oh, look here!'

She looked, and saw him drawing out a flat package, wrapped in paper: evidently a picture.

'A picture!' she cried.

He unwrapped the thing, and handed it to her. It was Theodor Worpswede's Still-leben: not very large, painted on a board.

Alexander (as we call him now) had, while looking for Hannele in Munich, seen his doll in a shop-window; but before he could make up his mind to buy it, it disappeared—sold. So where it was remained a question. Then he happened on the Still-leben, and, though he says he didn't know why, bought it.

Hannele looked at it, and went pale.

Some remarks about it, and some questions and answers relevant to the doll, passed between them, but, in the tumult of the waters and with the glacier there ahead of them, they didn't join battle there and then; but battle was clearly imminent. Anger flashed out between them when it started to rain and Alexander said: 'It is a pity you left your big coat down below.'

'What is the good of saying so now!' she replied, pale at the nose with anger.'

'Quite,' he said, as his eyes glowed and his brow blackened. 'What good suggesting anything at any time, apparently!'

We reflect that he would never have spoken to his wife in this way. His range of tones with Hannele is incomparably less limited and controlled. And hers with him shows very much greater diversity.

She turned round on him in the rain, as they stood perched nearly at the summit of that slanting hill-climb, with a glacier-paw hung almost invisible above, and waters gloating aloud in the gulf below.

Hostilities were open between them now. And the consequence in her of the sharp exchange of words meant to hurt, condemn and humiliate was that, having asked herself what he wanted to bully her into, she concluded:

He wanted her to love him. And he was offended, mortally offended because she had sold his doll.

And this conclusion 'made her feel quite warm to him, as they walked in the rain'. Since the senses in which she intended 'offend' as well as 'love' (which is the important word) misrepresented Alexander basically, a great deal remained for him to do before the end of the day—which is the end of the *nouvelle*. Actually, he doesn't get the assurance that he has successfully communicated his essential insight to Hannele—convinced her of its rightness— until he is about to leave her in the hotel by the lakeside at Kaprun. We don't, however, feel that her grasp of it, or it of her, is therefore shaky.

At one point in this episode of open battle she had retorted:

'Haven't I waited for you to suggest something? And all you can do is to come here with a picture to reproach me for having sold your doll. Ha! I'm glad I sold it. . . . What should I do but sell it. Why should I keep it, do you imagine?'
'Why do you come here with me to-day, then?'
'Why do I come here with you to-day?' she replied.
'I come to see the mountains, which are wonderful, and give me strength. And I come to see the glacier. Do you think I come here to see *you*? Why should I? You are always in some hotel or other away below.'
'You came to see the glacier *with* me,' he replied.

He put the stress here, regarding the glacier-excursion, in the significant place, as she can't have failed to realize. The joint project had clearly emerged with something like spontaneity between them, they having both so deep an awareness of the vital reality which their relation had, and of the need to promote clarifying development. They let the overt battle die down now, and no one who saw them climbing the last stretch to the glacier-head, and responding to the marvel of that static ice-flow could have safely assumed anything about them but that they had come to see the glacier *with* one another. When Alexander climbed laboriously till he could stand, at his peril, on the more or less flat surface,

Hannele watched from below, and saw the ridiculous exhibition, and was frightened and amused, but more frightened. And she kept calling, to the great joy of the Austrians down below:
'Come back. Do come back.'

Alexander didn't risk opening hostilities again—to probe was more than to risk it—till they were well on the way down again to Kaprun, sitting on a seat, in the early dusk, outside the restaurant of the terminus hotel, waiting for the car that had brought them there. He showed good judgment in taking his opportunity:

'Do you think,' said Alexander, 'you will marry the Herr Regierungsrat?'

The dialogue that starts with this question needs to be re-read in its unreduced fulness, not merely in the context of the unreduced tale, but in any reduction such as this which aims at a more perceptively responsive reading of the complete *nouvelle*. The fact is that the force of Lawrence's maxim, 'art-speech is the only speech,' is peculiarly obvious here: every elimination of a transition in speech-tone, or of some 'irrelevance' that looks merely incidental, or of graded evasiveness in responses to challenge, mars the felicity which is precision of thought and finality of demonstration. But to *say* this is the only possible corrective measure; so we go on as before.

She looked round, making wide eyes.
'It looks like it, doesn't it?' she said.
'Quite,' he said.
Hannele watched the woolly white dog. So of course it came wagging its ever-amiable hindquarters towards her. She looked at it still, but did not touch it.
'What makes you ask such a question,' she said.
'I can't say. But even so you haven't really answered. Do you really and fully intend to marry the Herr Regierungsrat? Is that your final intention at this moment?'

Of course, the response he gets isn't 'really' an answer, but an evasion.

He was silent for some moments. The huge woolly dog stood in front of him and breathed enticingly, with its tongue out. He only looked at it blankly.

'Well,' he said, 'if you were not going to marry the Herr Regierungsrat, I should suggest that you marry me.'

She stared away at the auto-garage, a very faint look of amusement, or pleasure, or ridicule on her face: or all three. And a certain shyness.

Her reaction is obviously complex, though anger plays no part in it—as yet. But she probably knows deep down, without being fully conscious of it, that when the word 'love' enters into the colloquy, anger will enter too. She proceeds to bring it in, relevantly to the question she has asked as to why he suggests marriage. He has parried her 'Why?' with another question: for what reason does a man usually ask a woman to marry him?'

Because he really loves her, I suppose. That seems to me the only excuse for a man asking a woman to marry him.

There is no getting further without the flash of lightning and the break of overt hostilities. Alexander can hardly believe that his tact would be successful.

'Leaving aside the question of whether you love me or I love you—' he began.

'I certainly *won't* leave it aside,' she said.

'And I certainly won't consider it,' he said, just as obstinately.

She turned now and looked full at him, with amazement, ridicule and anger in her face.

'I really think you must be mad,' she said.

'I doubt if you do think that,' he replied. 'It is only a method of retaliation, that is. I think you understand my point very clearly.'

That seems to me too large an assumption, in so far as he really entertained it. But if he entertained hope, as he clearly did—and very strongly, he had to go by this way, and his situation determined the mode of attack. Actually Hannele comes to a clear understanding of his 'point' when her will to resist gives in and her reluctance to agree yields to recognition of the truth of what he has put in front of her.

He took his knapsack from under the seat between his feet. And from the knapsack he took the famous picture.

'When,' he said, 'we were supposed to be in love with one another, you made that doll of me, didn't you?' And he sat looking at the odious picture.

As the altercation proceeds—and it *is* an altercation, a fact that in itself is significant, reminding us as it does of Ursula's burst of anger with Birkin in the chapter called 'Excuse'—it bears out Alexander's conclusion which is the 'point' he wants to get recognized by Hannele:

'All this about love,' he said, 'is very confusing, and very complicated.'

In the course of the militant exchange, he throws out a formulation which suggests what is to be objected to in the 'love' that Hannele demands as her right.

'I realized,' he said, 'that I had always made a mistake, undertaking to love.'
'It must have been an undertaking for *you*,' she cried.

Hannele implies that she is entitled to the undertaking, and that it is a failure in Alexander not to have undertaken to love her.

It helps the altercation to achieve the advances represented by bold and blunt utterance that it takes place at this stage in a swerving swift-moving car. Hannele is thrown with unseemly lack of decorum now against the driver, next to whom her place is, and now against Alexander, who sits on the other side of her.

'Honour, and obedience: and the proper physical feelings,' he said. 'To me that is marriage. Nothing else.'
'But what are the proper feelings but love?' asked Hannele.

They have now come to the terminus at Kaprun, and, walking on through the trees by the lake, have sat down on a seat.

'No,' he said. 'A woman wants you to adore her, and be in love with her—and I shan't. I will not do it again, if I live a monk for the rest of my days. I will neither adore you nor be in love with you.'

Actually he is defining the kind of mutual love on which a permanent relation can be based:

If a woman honours me—absolutely from the bottom of her nature honours me—and obeys me because of that, I take it, my desire for her goes very much deeper than if I was in love with her, or if I adored her.

*   *   *

And you can say what you like, but any woman today, no matter *how* much she loves her man—she could start any minute and make a doll of him. And her doll would be her hero: and her hero would be no more than her doll. My wife might have done. She did do it, in her mind. She had her doll of me right enough. Why, I heard her talk about me to other women. And her doll was a great deal sillier than the one you made. But it's all the same. If a woman loves you, she'll make a doll out of you. She'll never be satisfied till she's made your doll. And when she's got your doll, that's all she wants. And that's what love means.

'That's all she wants'—it isn't strictly fair to Hannele; she wanted more than that: a fact that is testified to by Alexander's favourable implicit judgment of her as being worth the difficult effort at bringing her round to a more adequate conception of love—a judgment that the tale, the power of Lawrence's 'art-speech', doesn't permit us to call paradoxical. There *is* paradox in the assimilation of her to the 'little lady', between whom and her there is sharp essential contrast. But what the challenge does is to bring out the much subtler paradox of Hannele's making the doll of the admired and awe-inspiring Captain. 'Hate is not the opposite of love. The real opposite of love is individuality.' What both Hannele and Mitchka in the opening of the tale are impressed by is the potent individuality of the Captain. The very first paragraph intimates that the making of the doll must involve taking liberties: 'She was doing something to the knee of the mannikin, so that the poor little gentleman flourished head downwards with arms widely tossed out.' But the essential paradox entails a conscious emphasis on the impressive distinction:

The face was beautifully modelled, and a wonderful portrait, dark-skinned, with a little, close-cut, dark moustache, and wide-open dark eyes, and that air of aloofness and perfect diffidence which marks an officer and a gentleman.

It is Mitchka who, all innocently, registers the inescapable element of irony:

Exactly him. Just as finished as he is. Just as complete. He is just like that: finished off.

'Exactly him', 'finished', 'complete', 'finished off'—at our first introduction to the doll we are not allowed to miss the paradox.

It is significant that Hannele, we are soon to be told, should ask herself why she had made it. She had made it, of course, with her artist's talent as a tribute to his individuality. But if life is individuality, the life-flow in the Captain is very strong; his presence is 'incalculable'. The unknown enters with life freely at the well-head, and her sense of that is what makes him irresistible to Hannele. The visual effects that are possible in the most wonderfully life-like doll can't—in spite of the 'wide-open dark eyes'—render what makes the incalculable life in him affect her so with vitalizing wonder.

Hannele was most uneasy because she seemed to have forgotten him in the three days whilst he had been away. He seemed to have disappeared out of her.

But when she heard his voice on the stairs, she 'knew there *was* something there.'

We are also told—told at the same time—that 'she was afraid again'. And we have a pointer here to the underlying significance of the uneasiness, the self-suspicion, implicit in her asking herself why she had made the doll. You know where you are with what is 'finished off'. Hannele of course was incapable of willing consciously to suppress the formidable mystery, the male incalculableness, she found so impressive in the Captain. Is it not there in the doll? It's there!—the wide-open dark eyes most certainly *are* there. But she has made a doll of him—as every woman, Alexander tells her, is ready to make a doll of her man. And when the Captain's doll becomes a figure in Theodor Worpswede's Still-leben the stillness of the unliving is emphasized. Hannele, when she turned her face from the picture 'as a cat turns its nose away from a lighted cigarette', betrayed an uneasy sense that she deserved to be held, in some unspecified way, at least suspect. As for Alexander's bracketing her with her female opposite, his wife, who made no literal dolls, it had its point. The little lady did indeed make a metaphorical doll of her husband, which in denying him the strong individuality as a male that characterizes him, merely served her stupid, petty and confident ego. Hannele (like Ursula) was *not* stupid, and the shockingly gross instance, of which the bearing ('offensively' insisted on) was plain, certainly told in the sudden surrender at the close—the tacit withdrawal of her refusal to see the validity of Alexander's insistence on the confusions engendered by the word 'love' and, positively, on the conditions of a permanent union.

Hannele certainly knows that he loves her, and he himself actually uses in a positive way the word 'love' on the penultimate page:

'Well,' he said slowly, 'she'll be my wife, and I shall treat her as such. If the marriage service says love and cherish—well, in that sense I shall do so.'

'Oh!' cried Hannele. 'What, *love* her? Actually love the poor thing?'

'Not in that sense of the word, no. I shan't adore her or be in love with her. But she'll be my wife, and I shall love and cherish her as such.'

'Just because she's your wife. Not because she's herself. Ghastly fate for any miserable woman,' said Hannele.

'I don't think so. I think it's her highest fate.'

'To be your wife?'

'To be a wife—and to be loved and shielded as a wife—not as a flirting woman.'

In my one-volume collection of the tales there are thirty-six lines left before the end of 'The Captain's Doll.' Hannele is a spirited woman, and even though she loves Alexander and profoundly (we see) trusts him, we wonder how the tale is to be brought to an end both inevitable in terms of the thought and compellingly natural. We find that the answer exemplifies the advantage, if you are a great novelist and D. H. Lawrence, of tackling a major human theme that challenges basic thought in a—*as* a—*nouvelle*.

As they were rowing in silence over the lake, he said: 'I shall leave tomorrow.'

She made no answer. She sat and watched the lights of the villa draw near. And then she said: 'I'll come to Africa with you. But I won't promise to honour and obey you.'

'I don't want you otherwise,' he said, very quietly. The boat was drifting to the little landing stage. Hannele's friends were hallooing to her from the balcony.

'Hallo!' she cried. 'Ja. Da bin ich. Ja, 's war wunderschön.'

Then to him she said:

'You'll come in?'

'No,' he said, 'I'll row straight back.'

From the villa they were running down the steps to meet Hannele.
'But won't you have me even if I love you?' she asked him.
'You must promise the other,' he said. 'It comes in the marriage
service.'
  'Hat's geregnet? Wie war das Wetter? Warst du auf dem Gletscher?'
cried the voices from the garden.
  'Nein—kein Regen. Wunderschön! Ja, er war ganz auf dem
Gletscher,' cried Hannele in reply. And to him, *sotto voce*:
'Don't be a solemn ass. Do come in.'
  'No,' he said, 'I don't want to come in.'
  'Do you want to go away tomorrow? Go, if you *do*. But anyway, I
won't say it *before* the marriage service. I needn't, need I?'
  She stepped from the boat on to the plank.
  'Oh,' she said, turning round, 'give me that picture, please, will you?
I want to burn it.'

There are four further lines to leave us assured that this *is* the
quietly matter-of-fact but clinching inevitable end and upshot—a
wholly satisfying resolution. Hannele, intelligent as she is, couldn't
have brought her pride and habit to allow such a change to be so
easy—change to recognizing Alexander's good sense—but for the
voices shouting their questions from the garden, and the answers
coming so naturally from her: 'Nein, kein Regen. Wunderschön!
Ja, er war ganz auf dem Gletscher.' The implication of the tone
has a supporting context. Such an answer confirms her friends'
sense, and in confirming it confirms her own, that the relations
between her and Alexander which make the joint excursion to
the glacier so natural seem to point to the pair's becoming—the
pair they essentially are or are meant to be—formally and really
husband and wife.
  And actually the friction between them and their manner of
conveying it imply that they matter to one another as profoundly
as a man and a woman can. They are intimate with a reality far
more real than the intimacy of a pair of lovers intoxicated with
the passion of adoring love. The running altercation between them
is that of a man and a woman who essentially *want* to justify their
feeling that, between them, they have the qualities that might go
to form a permanent union of the right kind. The trouble of course
is that they differ as to what the right kind is. Alexander is equally
with Birkin confronted by the reflected image of the moon which
always re-forms when he has done his best to shatter and disperse it.

After a moment's silence she [Ursula] replied:
'But how can I, you don't love me! You only want your own ends.
You don't want to serve me, and yet you want me to serve you. It is
so one-sided!'

The firmness of Hannele's refusal is of the same order, and expresses itself in the same way, though it is undermined by incipient
intuition:

But because he gave himself away, she forgave him. And the strange
passion of his, that gave out incomprehensible flashes, *was* rather
fascinating to her. She felt just a tiny bit sorry for him. But she wasn't
going to be bullied by him. She wasn't going to give in to him and his
black passion. No, never. For love on equal terms she was quite ready.
She only waited for him to offer it.

She waited in vain. What she called 'love on equal terms' went
with the self-ignorance that made her ask uneasily *what* had
moved her to make the doll of Alexander. Both the doll and the
demand for 'love on equal terms' are expressions of the female ego:
the flatteringness of the doll and the plausibility of the demand are
specious; they cover resentment at the male strength that went
with the mystery in Alexander—the profound vital maleness that
Hannele, in her complex reaction, so admired in him and that
made her at the root of herself, for all his disconcertingness, trust
him as she did. She came (but pulled up) to the brink of marrying
the Herr Regierungsrat because his way of kissing her hand made
her feel 'like a queen in exile'. But when the Captain reappears her
profounder being at once decides for *him*. This is what gives its
distinctive meaning to the glacier-excursion *with one another*—
which has for end of the enacted drama the accordant and significant outcome. The friction and running altercation confirm in
him the lesson of the 'love'-marriage with the little lady; it is for
the man in especial to cultivate his singleness and to devote himself
to some creative purpose that the deeper, the non-ego promptings
of his individuality impel him to, or there will be no prosperous
final union.

Every human sameness is different; it couldn't occur to Birkin
to talk of the marriage service or to enjoin Ursula to honour and
obey. But the appropriateness of such terms and such talk when
Alexander is concerned to bring home to Hannele the kind of

finality he has in mind is triumphantly vindicated by 'The Captain's Doll'. The easy succession of her utterances is significant:

'Ja, er war ganz auf dem Gletscher,' cried Hannele in reply. And to him, *sotto voce*: 'Don't be a solemn ass. Do come in.'

She is merely showing how completely she has come to share his attitude and his sense of things, and that Hannele married won't be the less Hannele.

The tale ends on this sentence: 'He pulled back quickly into the darkness.' Such a close prompts us to observe that the darkness in Alexander is always close at hand and very accessible; that is for him a condition of the deep responsibility that distinguishes him—and so neither for this darkness has Hannele anything to fear. She knows it.

It is perhaps proper to insist after such an exercise, of which I am all too conscious of the clumsiness, that I have not been offering to define any thought that is *behind* the novel-long tale. The tale itself *is* the thought; my clumsy commentary is meant as an aid to perceiving that the delicate perfection of Lawrence's art-speech can be duly appreciated only as the precision and completeness of the thinking.

V

'THE RAINBOW'

NOTHING important can really be said simply—simply *and* safely; and by 'safely' I mean so as to ensure that the whole intuited apprehension striving to find itself, to discover what it is in words, is duly served, and not thwarted. It takes a context, often a subtly and potently creative one, to do that. I have insisted a good deal that, while 'life' is a necessary word, life is concretely 'there' only in the living individual being. This might seem obvious enough; but Lawrence, with good reason, was intensely conscious that what ought to have been a truism was, with ever-increasing callousness or blankness, ignored by the very spirit of our humane civilization.

It doesn't at all follow that he tended to inculcate anything in the nature of individualistic self-sufficiency. He was a great creative writer; no writer with any claim to greatness could have served that spirit. But Lawrence, possessed by his sense of the desperate need, in a neo-Benthamite world, to emphasize that what submitted to statistical treatment couldn't possibly be life, took his developed thought decidedly further than my isolated sentence intimates—took it into what goes inseparably with the emphasis on individuality; took it into explicitness about the 'inseparably'. It is human life he is dealing with in the following passage, and we can say that if the thought savours ostensibly of paradox, it certainly commands assent.

As a fixed object, even as an individuality or a personality, no human being, man or woman, amounts to much. The great I AM does not apply to human beings, so they may as well leave it alone. As soon as anybody, man or woman, becomes a great I AM, he becomes nothing. Man or woman, each is a flow, a flowing life. And without one another, we can't flow, just as a river cannot flow without banks. A woman is one bank of the river of my life, and the world is the other. Without the two shores, my life would be a marsh. It is the relationship to woman, and to my fellow-men, which makes me myself a river of life.

And it is this even that gives me my soul. A man who has never had a vital relationship to any other human being doesn't really have a soul. We cannot feel that Immanuel Kant ever had a soul. A soul is something that forms and fulfils itself in my contacts, my living touch with people I have loved or hated or truly known. I am born with the clue to my soul. The wholeness of my soul I must achieve. And by my soul I mean my wholeness.

Such a passage prompts one to remark that there is more to be said of Lawrence's thought about life, his essential original thought, than we have yet taken note of. I can't help asking myself whether, in saying that life is concretely 'there' only in the living individual being, I imply an oversimplified distinction between 'concrete' and 'abstract.' 'Life' is certainly a necessary word; and that *Women in Love* deals with the development, actual and potential, of English life is a necessary proposition. Is it tenable that in this proposition the word 'life' points to something merely abstract? What it points to is surely concrete in that it couldn't have been made present for thought—and even in illusory ostensibleness—by externally descriptive-selective means in a discursive way; hence the importance and originality of *Women in Love* as thought. What this book is 'about' is *created* in the creative writer's thinking, and yet it is not arbitrary. It is 'there', challengingly, a complex undeniable identity—as what is portended by the word 'life' in the Tripos formula, 'Life and Thought', is not. It is creatively 'there', realized by the evocative genius 'at the maximum of his imagination', and to say 'realized' is to give a felicitous force to that verb. For Lawrence may be said to create realities; he at any rate makes thought possible, about 'English life' as thought about the real, in the only way that can be seriously suggested.

The Rainbow and *Women in Love* are intimately related, but surprisingly unlike—though they are both obviously by D. H. Lawrence. Lawrence writes to Edward Garnett in a letter dated 30 December, 1913: 'In a few days' time I shall send you the first half of *The Sisters*—which I should rather call *The Wedding Ring*— . . . It is very different from *Sons and Lovers*: written in another language almost.' *The Sisters*, one is told, is what became *Women in Love*, though I am bound to question whether in this instance it became anything but *The Rainbow*. Probably, when Lawrence threw out the other suggested title for it, it hadn't wholly emerged as itself from the one projected novel on which Lawrence had embarked, and of which he wrote to A. D. McLeod in April 1913: 'I am doing a novel which I have never grasped. Damn its eyes, there I am at page 145, and I've no notion what it's about. I hate it. F. says it is good. But it's like a novel in a foreign language I don't know very well—I can only just make out what it is about.'

This is not affectation, but an emphatic way of describing the emergence, as he experienced it, of original thought out of the ungrasped apprehended—the intuitively, the vaguely but insistently apprehended: first the stir of apprehension, and then the prolonged repetitious wrestle to persuade it into words. We have the two novels that separated out in the organic working of that first creative impulsion: *The Rainbow* and *Women in Love*. And of the later book he might have said: 'It is *very* different from *The Rainbow*: written in another language almost.' We can only marvel at the rapidity with which his genius developed. Both books are incredibly original. He said justly (where at least the achieved was in question) to Edward Marsh in a letter dated 6 November 1915: 'You jeered rather at *The Rainbow*, but notwithstanding it is a big book. I tell you, who know.' Of *Women in Love* we can guess pretty shrewdly that he didn't doubt it to be capable of standing by itself and to be the greater achievement. And if he wrote in a letter, '*The Rainbow* and *Women in Love* are really an organic artistic whole,' that expresses his sense of their having emerged from the same creative intuition, and of his need to have written *The Rainbow* in order to tackle successfully his diagnostic and prophetic study of what was in 1914 contemporary England—and modern civilization.

The Rainbow clearly led up to *Women in Love*; we see well enough why Lawrence, in several letters, refers to the latter as a 'sequel' to *The Rainbow*. He looked back from his own time, and seeking to understand that, and whither England was tending or driving, asked what essential growth, what development, lay behind the present—which, as he lived in it, was becoming something else. He could hardly have written *The Rainbow* without at the same time shaping in the process a sequel—not merely an 'idea' of it, unless an idea can be concrete, and the forming idea be the creative writer's thought in its characteristically concrete formation. 'Art-speech is the only speech'—the only speech that can render living thought; and Lawrence's problem was how to achieve precision and cogency in that.

Though his present in *Women in Love* is, of its nature, dynamic, and, as such, straining urgently, and very responsive to impulsions of change, it is nevertheless a present—England now. The distinctive offer of *The Rainbow* is to render development concretely—the complex change from generation to generation and the inter-weaving of the generations. *His* present, which is nothing in the nature of a newspaper present, has to be created, and only a great genius could create it so that one had to agree: this *is* the present. And who questions (the 'who' is to be taken as interrogatory, so that—from my point of view—a questioner would probably expose himself to a placing comment) that *Women in Love* gives the present of a half-century ago? The England, the 'English life' evoked is of course selective; but so is any 'objectivity' that thought offers to bring in front of us. The question, where Lawrence is concerned, regards the criteria implicit in the reality he presents us with, and, in such a matter, they are peculiarly evasive when dealt with discursively; they elude analytic-descriptive generalities. It is in an immediate way that one is convinced; one's conviction is confirmed by thought, the life of which the process of confirmation at the same time nourishes. Of course there have been developments in half-a-century, but they go essentially to confirm Lawrence's insight; so that he remains the incomparable promoter of perception and judgment where *our* present is in question.

For all the marked difference in style between the two books, the implicit criteria, and something characteristic of the method of *Women in Love*, are what have been worked out in the writing of *The Rainbow*. The criteria are those of the great writer who said: 'At the maximum of our imagination we are religious.' As I remarked on one of the occasions on which I have quoted this utterance before, 'imagination' and 'religious' are important words in the context of Lawrence's thought, but as they stand in the isolated sentence they are far from unambiguous. Of course, reading them there in what we know to be a Laurentian maxim, we take the Laurentian charge they transmit. As good a way of intimating—that is, of achieving a due explicitness about—the nature of that charge as any, it seems to me, is to consider the case of Skrebensky, who is, in the last third of *The Rainbow*, the man in Ursula Brangwen's developing emotional life. Already in the chapter (XI) called 'First Love' we have this (pp. 308–9), which leaves us in no doubt as to his life-deficiency:

> He went about his duties, giving himself up to them. At the bottom of his heart his self, the soul that aspired and had true hope of self-effectuation lay as dead, still-born, a dead weight in his womb. Who was he, to hold important his personal connection? What did a man matter personally? He was just a brick in the whole great social fabric, the nation, the modern humanity. His personal movements were small, and entirely subsidiary. The whole form must be ensured, not ruptured for any personal reason whatsoever, since no personal reason could justify such a breaking. What did personal intimacy matter? One had to fill one's place in the whole, the great scheme of man's elaborate civilization, that was all. The whole mattered—but the unit, the person, had no importance, except as he represented the Whole. So Skrebensky left the girl out and went his way, serving what he had to serve, and enduring what he had to endure, without remark. To his own intrinsic life, he was dead. .... He had his five senses too. They were to be gratified.

It is made plain to us that he is not a mere vulgar cynic. He takes duty seriously, and duty for him is to 'the established order of things'. In fact, he serves to enforce the meaning of 'responsibility' in the profound Laurentian sense of the word—to enforce it by bringing out its immeasurable difference from anything suggested by 'duty'. It is made plain for us too that Skrebensky is not without some kind of awareness of the unmanning contradiction involved for him in his inner life. The effect on Ursula gives us a Laurentian theme that again plays a major part in *Women in Love*, this time as involved in the relations between Gudrun and Gerald Crich. It is a prolonged ordeal for both sisters—in *The Rainbow* the ordeal is Ursula's:

> So there came over Skrebensky a sort of nullity which more and more terrified Ursula. She felt there was something hopeless she had to submit to.

The adjective 'hopeless' is not a word that it is Lawrence's way anywhere to throw in slackly, as suggesting a vague intensity in the state vaguely deplored, and most certainly not in *The Rainbow*.

In the brief quoted passage it refers us to the title of the book. We all know that the rainbow is a symbol, and we associate it with promise and hope. But there is more in it than that, otherwise Lawrence wouldn't have made it the title of the novel that has for its sequel *Women in Love*. For in the title there is no irony, and in the sequel no changed Laurentian attitude. What I call 'attitude' here I qualify as Laurentian because it is basic to Lawrence's thought. True, what he makes of the symbol was potential in it; but the actual value, the complex significance, that Lawrence's novel creates for it and invests it with is distinctively and pregnantly Laurentian.

The attitude and tone can't be called optimistic, and how misleading it would be to lay the stress on hope and promise the following passage serves to intimate. I pick it from an essay in *Phoenix I* (p. 733) because it brings in the Ark with the rainbow:

Catastrophe alone never helped man. The only thing that ever avails is the living adventurous spark in the souls of men. If there is no living adventurous spark, then death and disaster are as meaningless as tomorrow's newspaper.

Take the fall of Rome. During the Dark Ages of the fifth, sixth, seventh centuries A.D., the catastrophes that befell the Roman Empire didn't alter the Romans a bit. They went on just the same, rather as we go on to-day, having a good time when they could get it, and not caring. Meanwhile Huns, Goths, Vandals, Visigoths, and all the rest wiped them out.

With what result? The flood of barbarism rose and covered Europe from end to end.

But bless your life, there was Noah in his Ark with the animals. There was young Christianity. There were the lonely fortified monasteries, like little arks floating and keeping the adventure afloat. There is no break in the great adventure in consciousness. Throughout the howling deluge, some few brave souls are steering the ark under the rainbow.

The monks and bishops of the Early Church carried the soul and spirit of man unbroken, unabated, undiminished over the howling flood of the Dark Ages. Then this spirit of undying courage was fused into the barbarians, in Gaul, in Italy, and the new Europe began. But the germ had never been allowed to die.

Once all men in the world lost their courage and their newness, the world would come to an end.

Not, then, just hope or the reassurance implicit in a promise that can be relied on because it is from God. The peace that Lawrence counsels us to seek and secure isn't that. Rather it is the peace of basic responsibility fully accepted—'responsibility' as the young ship's-captain of 'The Secret Sharer' so naturally assumed it as his. Responsibility in that profound sense goes with the imagination that makes possible a liberation from the imprisoning ego; it calls for the developed intelligence that (depending as it does on developed intuition) can make—if the courage is there— the individual being the disinterested servant of life. But Conrad's distinctive attitude and tone are such that, challenged to describe them as we have them in the work of his kindled imagination, one would hardly find oneself prompted to bring in, for any positive major use, the word 'religious'. Rather, it is Ramón of *The Plumed Serpent* who, in that early intimate exchange with Kate, describes in Laurentian terms what 'responsibility' implies as it actually prevails in Lawrence's art.

But we didn't create ourselves; and the sole access to the promptings to be gathered from the unknown—from which life and creativity enter us—is by the well-head, which is deep below our valid thought. Submission to the promptings is the escape from the ego and its will; but such submission is, of its nature, a very active matter, demanding self-knowledge, intensive cultivation of the most delicate intuitiveness, and the courage to arrive at conclusions the precision and finality of which are not guaranteed: the responsibility for them is ours, and where it is not taken up there is no genuine responsibility. 'But Noah, of course, is always in an unpopular minority'—it doesn't occur to Skrebensky to belong to that; that is, he leaves responsibility to the Whole, or to the community, or to the greatest good of the greatest number.

Ursula, who is no more than a girl learning about love and life, and committed (she is intelligent) to discovering what her own 'life-responsibility' dictates, is first, for all Skrebensky's young-love irresistibleness, made uneasy by her sense of his inner nullity as a man, and then, as she matures, brought to a decided placing judgment against him. The very end of the book gives us one of the two or three main quotable passages in it in which the rainbow symbol figures. The passage is essentially explicitness relating immediately to the significance of the symbol, and forms part of her reflections as she lies in bed recovering from an illness brought on by uncertainty, apprehension and emotional conflict.

In everything she saw she grasped and groped to find the creation of the living God, instead of the old, hard barren form of bygone living. Sometimes great terror possessed her. Sometimes she lost touch, she lost her feeling, she could only know the old horror of the husk which bound in her and all mankind. They were all in prison, they were all going mad.

*   *   *

... And then, in the blowing clouds, she saw a band of faint iridescence colouring in faint colours a portion of the hill. And forgetting, startled, she looked for the hovering colour and saw a rainbow forming itself. In one place it gleamed fiercely, and, her heart anguished with hope, she sought the shadow of iris where the bow should be. Steadily the colour gathered, mysteriously, from nowhere, it took presence upon itself, there was a faint, vast rainbow. The arc bended and strengthened itself till it arched indomitable, making great architecture of light and colour and the space of heaven, its pedestals luminous in the corruption of new houses on the low hill, its arch the top of heaven.
And the rainbow stood on the earth. She knew that the sordid people who crept hard-scaled and separate on the face of the world's corruption were living still, that the rainbow was arched in their blood ...

This is the form taken by Ursula's reaction against Skrebensky. To estimate its significance fairly we need to remind ourselves that Ursula is a major character in the sequel, *Women in Love*, too, and finally marries Birkin. Birkin, of course, is very different from Skrebensky; but then so is Ursula from Lawrence. It was Lawrence who created the complex charge of significance, the subtle value that fitted the symbol to be the title of his novel: Ursula's rainbow isn't Lawrence's.
I think (it is not an unrelated matter) of the difference between Ursula's fortune in love and Gudrun's. Birkin isn't a novelist or a poet; but he is nevertheless much more like Lawrence than Ramón of *The Plumed Serpent* is— *The Plumed Serpent*, 'the most important thing I have done so far'. The two fictional characters, Ramón and Birkin, are extremely unlike one another—extremely but not utterly; for they have this in common: they have both revolted

129

THOUGHT, WORDS AND CREATIVITY

against the enclosed ego and attained to human responsibility. Lawrence stresses the feminine in the title—and more than the title—of *Women in Love*; that is necessary to his insistence that the ideas of equality and inequality are irrelevant—and worse, the relevant stress falling on *difference*, and the difference being essential to life (and not merely, in humanity, to the biological continuance of the species).

Ursula is an intelligent girl of strong character and proper pride. Her reaction against Skrebensky has a Laurentian significance; it leads up to the battle that is an important constituent in the chapter called 'Moony' and the later chapter called 'Excurse'. Birkin is very unlike Skrebensky; though without Skrebensky's charm, he is far from being a spiritual nullity. He is the man who, though he would like to save Gerald from his mechanistic fate, and have him for his friend, diagnoses Gerald's disease and sees him as modern civilization speeding towards the death-break—the cessation of life (which is creativity) in a 'frozen world'. In fact, he shares Lawrence's diagnostic insight. He shares, too, Lawrence's view of the difference between woman and man. The immediately necessary point is made, I think, when I quote again from 'Moony' this (*Women in Love* page 262–3):

'I always think I am going to be loved—and then I am let down. You *don't* love me, you know. You don't want to serve me. You only want yourself.'

A shiver of rage went over his veins at this repeated: 'You don't want to serve me.' All the paradisal disappeared from him. 'No,' he said, irritated, 'I don't want to serve you, because there is nothing there to serve. What you want me to serve is nothing, mere nothing. It isn't even you, it is your mere female quality. And I wouldn't give a straw for your female ego—it's a rag doll.'

Birkin speaks in exasperation, for in fact he truly and profoundly loves her. He is exasperated at the hopelessness of trying to talk her into conviction. 'It must happen beyond the sound of words.' It is a question of what love is and what marriage should be; and actually she is brought to recognize the force of his point and tacitly admit conversion—brought to it merely by the genuineness and power of what he is.

She is luckier than her sister Gudrun. Gudrun is attracted by Gerald Crich's male beauty and the masterfulness of his organizing talent and will; and then repelled by the emptiness of his intrinsic being—just as Ursula had been by Skrebensky's conventional nullity—as a centre of life. It is for the man to foster in himself openness, necessarily creative, to the unknown—to strive towards free, unbiased and uncommitted receptivity at the well-head; his living spiritual authority is a matter of that. The woman driven to conclude that he is null reacts as Ursula and Gudrun do. Gudrun wants prestige and power, but, in the proximity of the chilling fact of death, discovers the vacuum in Gerald where she looked for the creative living centre—discovers too that she can't forgive the lack in a man she might, possibly, have otherwise thought of as hers. Her reaction is to fall back on the bullying superiority of Loerke, the artist-cynic.

I have been exemplifying how impossible it is, in an attempted expository treatment of Lawrence's thought, to achieve an expository ordering. This is not to offer an adverse criticism, but to bear involuntary testimony to the wholeness, the organic unity, inseparable in Lawrence's thought from his distinctive emphasis on life. My last point regarded both the difference and the relations between woman and man. I was about to go back to the problem of doing justice to the pregnancy, in the title of the book, of the symbolic rainbow, when I remembered that Ursula's mother, Anna, had, in introspective self-questioning, Ursula being then a new-born baby, herself dwelt expansively on the symbol. When I looked up the place in Chapter VI, 'Anna Victrix', I was reminded further that Will Brangwen, her husband, was involved too—in a way that gave significance to their quarrel (for it amounted to that) about Lincoln Cathedral.

This is the passage from 'Anna Victrix'; it gives us an essential element in the total Laurentian charge—the charge that explains why the novel was called *The Rainbow*:

Anna loved the child very much, oh, very much. Yet still she was not quite fulfilled. She had a slight expectant feeling, as of a door half opened. Here she was, safe and still in Cossethay. But she felt as if she were not in Cossethay at all. She was straining her eyes to something beyond. And from her Pisgah mount, which she had attained, what could she see? A faint, gleaming horizon, a long way off, and a rainbow like an archway, a shadow-door with faintly coloured coping above it. Must she be moving thither?

Something she had not, something she did not grasp, could not arrive at. There was something beyond her. But why must she start on the journey? She stood so safely on the Pisgah mountain.

★   ★   ★

Dawn and sunset were the feet of the rainbow that spanned the day, and she saw the hope, the promise. Why should she travel any further? (page 183).

Her husband's 'sense of something more' (for he had such a sense, though there is no rainbow for him) is different; the rainbow is hers. We say this to ourselves because it is pretty obvious that we are meant to: it is not for nothing that the page or so evoking him ends immediately before the just-quoted passage begins. The juxtaposition is significant.

This is Will Brangwen (page 181):

And what more? What more would be necessary? The great mass of activity in which mankind was engaged meant nothing to him. By nature he had no part in it. What did he live for, then? For Anna only, and for the sake of living? What did he want on this earth? Anna only, and his children, and his life with his children and her? Was there no more?

He was attended by a sense of something more, something further, which gave him absolute being. It was as if now he existed in Eternity, let Time be what it might. What was there outside?

'Nothing': that is the answer assumed. This is plain from the way in which Will, in the next chapter ('The Cathedral'), the substance of which precedes chronologically what happens in the chapter just quoted from, reacts when Anna asserts, and sticks to it, that she doesn't accept the significance he imputes to Lincoln Cathedral. She too is filled with awe at the marvel of the interior; and so also is Lawrence himself, as is shown in the sustained power of the prose in which he evokes the marvel: words will do this only when the charged and possessed imagination of the great artist informs them. But in the wonderfully controlled ecstatic prose there is something that, when it asserts itself, makes the ecstasy specifically Will Brangwen's, as it does explicitly here (page 190) — triggering off rebellion in Anna:

And there was no time nor life nor death, but only this, this timeless consummation, where the thrust from earth met the thrust from earth and the arch was locked on the keystone of ecstasy. This was all, this was everything. Till he came to himself in the world below. Then again he gathered himself together, in transit, every jet of him strained and leaped, leaped clear into the darkness above, to the fecundity and the unique mystery, to the touch, the clasp, the consummation, the climax of eternity, the apex of the arch.

But—of Anna—there follows this:

She too was overcome, but silenced rather than tuned to the place. She loved it as a world not quite her own, she resented his transports and ecstasies. His passion in the cathedral at first awed her, then made her angry.

She remembered that the open sky was no blue vault, and told herself protestingly that it was shut out. And she taunted Will with the faces carved where possible by the irreverent masons:

These sly little faces peeped out of the grand tide of the cathedral like something that knew better. They knew quite well, these little imps that retorted on man's own illusion, that the cathedral was not absolute. They winked and leered, giving suggestion of the many things that had been left out of the great concept of the church.

This, of course, is Lawrence himself—our awareness of that is overriding, without our being disabled from accepting it as Anna. 'God burned no more in that bush': that, extracted from the prose of the context, with which it doesn't quarrel, is close to speech— which might be either's.

The tensions that complicate the married life of Will and Anna (it was a 'love-marriage') are dealt with by a novelist of first-hand perception and rare powers of subtle thought. The difference that sparks between them on the visit to Lincoln Cathedral is one of them; but my immediate concern with it is the help it gives towards 'defining' the charge of 'value', the significance, that Lawrence creates for the rainbow of his chosen title. Anna, in her creative sense, her apprehension, of the rainbow in the chapter, 'Anna Victrix', makes it something more complex than simply hope and promise: 'She was straining her eyes to something beyond . . . Something she had not, something she could not grasp, could not arrive at.' And it is through Anna that Lawrence registers his self-dissociation from Will's way of being religious. Whatever the way in which the adjective applies to Lawrence's sense and service of the unknown, these amount to something fundamentally other than Will's cult of the cathedral and what the cathedral represents.

It seems to me that Lawrence's basic attitude is religious in the most vital, the most living, way: it is the way compelled by a properly indocile perception of what our civilization is doing to life. It contrasts not only with Will Brangwen's; it contrasts equally with T. S. Eliot's—as these sentences announce ambiguously (they were written long before the first of the *Four Quartets*):

We derive from the unknown, and we result into the unknown. But for us the beginning is not the end; for us the two are not one.

Lawrence believes in the reality of time, for he believes in the reality of development and essential change—the appearance in the universe of what didn't exist before. For him the relation between the creator and created life is utterly unlike what it is for Eliot—but then for Lawrence the unknowable supreme principle and potency and life itself are utterly unlike Eliot's God and Eliot's mankind.

The brief implicitly anti-Eliotic utterance I have quoted comes from an essay in *Phoenix I* (page 695) entitled 'Life', in which Lawrence is explicit about man's unique status as he envisages it.

Midway between the beginning and the end is man, midway between that which creates and that which is created, midway in another world, partaking of both, yet transcending.

All the while man is referred back. He cannot create himself. At no moment can man create himself. He can but submit to the creator, to the primal unknown out of which issues the all. At every moment we issue like a balanced flame from the primal unknown. We are not self-contained or self-accomplished. At every moment we issue from the unknown.

To be a great creative writer, born in England, at Eastwood, of a miner's family, at that moment in history, was for a Lawrence to find himself committed to a prophetic role. He was impelled inevitably, by his astonishing gifts, into a questioning examination of the deepest underlying conditions of civilized life. Was the continuance of civilization in the spirit of its modern accelerating development possible? Wasn't overt human disaster certainly ahead, and not far distant, and essential human disaster already upon us? Thus his preoccupation with human responsibility and the relation of man to the unknown was everywhere urgent and insistent; it was in and of the creative drive behind his thought and art. This *was*, to invoke his own injunction, to cultivate 'consciousness'.

It is all in keeping that Lawrence in various places gives us some explicitness about the nature of responsibility and (it follows) of the self-discipline it calls for. In the essay, 'Life', for instance, we have this suggestive paragraph:

I turn my face, which is blind and yet which knows, like a blind man turning to the sun, I turn my face to the unknown, which is the beginning, and like a blind man who lifts his face to the sun I know the sweetness of the influx from the source of creation into me. Blind, forever blind, yet knowing, I receive the gift, I know myself the ingress of the creative unknown. Like a seed, which unknowing receives the sun and is made whole, I open onto the great warmth of primal creativity and begin to be fulfilled.

Responsibility involves scrupulous delicacy of apprehension at the well-head, and therefore the cultivation of natural aptitude and delicate scruple.

We shall never know what is the beginning. We shall never know how it comes to pass that we have form and being. But we may always know how through the doorways of the spirit and the body enters the vivid unknown, which is made known in us. Who comes, who is it that we hear outside in the night? Who knocks, who knocks again? Who is it that unlatches the painful door?

Then behold, there is something new in our midst. We blink our eyes, we cannot see. We lift the lamp of previous understanding, we illuminate the stranger with the light of our established knowledge. Then at last we accept the newcomer, he is enrolled among us.

The image, 'seed', in 'like a seed' helps in the business of evocative definition. The seed responds livingly to sun and moisture because, we say, it is potential life itself—and we rest too easily, in blank assumption, on the assumed value of the word 'potential'. Let us say, rather, that the life in the seed is asleep; it can certainly die.

But when it wakes, and develops in the warmth of the sun, it develops to an old pattern; we don't expect a mutation. What we are concerned with now is newness. The seed analogy holds in so far as it suggests that the man in whom his attained and realized 'manhood' is active *is* life, pre-eminently life, on our side of the well-head, and so is especially quick—let us bear in mind Lawrence's archaic use of the word—to apprehend the new life-promptings from the unknown, whence life enters us. But the stranger is new, and the newness and 'our established knowledge' have to accommodate themselves to each other. There is no absolute certainty and no finality; for, even if there is no growth, no change, in the unknown, the most scrupulous constatation may contain error.

Justified near-certitude regarding the new involves, as life does, creativity. The creativity in me isn't mine—it doesn't belong to me; yet I am responsible for what it does. Is, then, what it takes a master of 'art-speech' to constate 'objective'? Well, it means to be; how far it is (or isn't) is left to me to judge; it is my responsibility—which may take, as where Lawrence was concerned, a very long time to discharge to one's satisfaction. 'Verifiable' has a different meaning in regard to judgments about life from what it has for the scientist.

Major creative writers are rare: I put it in this way, because the newly apprehended at the well-head, to affect a culture, must be realized in producible thought. And even so, producible and (one would think) overwhelming, it may make little difference; what difference has Lawrence made? In writing it, I meant this question as rhetorical, but feel now that it had better be, just a little, an inquiry too. Lawrence succeeded in making a living for himself and Frieda with his pen: his art in the short stories and the tales was compelling, but it appears to me very possible that his novels were read for the misunderstood characteristics that earned him a name for immorality. In any case his thought (and that is his art) was in general—I include myself in the generalization—uncomprehended, it was basically too new and important.

And yet it is perhaps too early to say that he made no difference. Perhaps the confidence of such a judgment reveals a certain crudity of assumption about the way in which a dynamism like Lawrence's could work. There has undoubtedly been a change for the worse in cultural conditions since he died, a change that might seem to make any hope that he could tell as an influence on the prevailing culture merely ridiculous. The forming of such an intellectual community as he irradiated at Eastwood, was life-centre to, and drew life from, is in today's conditions inconceivable. He was launched as an author with astonishing ease, and found little in the way of making the kinds of contact he needed: he couldn't doubt that there was still an influential educated public in England. Yet the prospects of civilization, as he saw them, were not cheerful, but distinctly chilling: the paragraph I printed as epigraph to my last book, *The Living Principle*, represented his profound conviction:

I knew then, and I know now, it is no use trying to do anything – I speak only for myself – publicly. It is no use trying merely to modify present forms. The whole great form of our era will have to go.

The first sentence, it is true, regarded the war which made Horatio Bottomley a power in England; but 'I know then' is followed by 'and I know now'; so it doesn't regard merely that. Lawrence was convinced that England – and he was right – hadn't begun to recover, and wouldn't. How could it? The war accelerated the drive of modern civilization that Birkin, in *Women in Love*, sees as irresistible. Birkin, however, doesn't the less fight with all his being against the irresistible drive. Nor does Lawrence. In spite of his saying, 'It is no use trying to do anything . . . in public', what more could anyone do, and do in a public way, than carry on war against the disease with that marvellous output of books and essays and tales? The life in him was something like unshaken invincible faith; it affirmed itself, and was the proof of the affirmation; he couldn't have believed at a deep level that such implicitly affirming creativity was doomed to make no difference.

Wasn't it this difficult faith, this paradoxical quasi-hope, that Lawrence's rainbow symbolized for him as the upshot of his novel? The Laurentian rainbow meant faith-in-life overhung by frightening menace – menace yoked, for the 'conscious', with a paradoxical contradiction. The novel offers to bring before us the immediate past of the England of *Women in Love*. The generation it starts with is Tom Brangwen's, who is the old rural England.

But already the embanked canal, carried along the valley, has shut off the farm from the industrialized world it now supplies. Brangwen needs no rainbow; his problem is to find the woman with whom to make a life together. Simply, sanely and touchingly (which means convincingly), he solves his problem: he and the Polish lady, with such different backgrounds, have little in common except that they attract one another, and, for all the difference between them, are both such that they can trust the intuitive conviction that the other will be the right life-long mate. In this respect, though she is a lady and knows the outside world—both very important facts, they answer to this part of the account of the characteristic Brangwen husband and wife: 'They were two very separate beings, vitally connected, knowing nothing of each other, yet living in their separate ways from one root.'

We have here what serves as a foil (not a wholly felicitous word, yet the other, 'norm', that suggests itself seems a good deal more unsuitable) against which the tensions and miseries attendant on the growing complexity of the conditions of life in the two succeeding generations are set off. The marriage between Will and Anna, the wholly Polish girl, is a young-love match that Tom Brangwen knows it would be useless to forbid, and I have already dealt with the friction that soon manifests itself between husband and wife. As for her rainbow vision (page 183), which meant not merely hope or promise, but 'straining her eyes to something beyond', we know: 'She did not turn to her husband, for him to lead her.' Also: 'And soon again she was with child. Which made her satisfied, and took away her discontent.' And further: 'With satisfaction, she relinquished the adventure to the unknown. She was bearing her children.'—'She was a door and a threshold, she herself.' A relevant, and very important point, about the difference between woman and man is made here.

Ursula, her daughter, cares so much about 'responsibility', which she knows intuitively and by experience in the family (there's her 'grandfather', Tom Brangwen) is the business of the man, that she can't forgive Skrebensky his complete and shameless lack of it. Ursula, then, has character and distinction. They ensure her a wide experience in the world of her time; experience—the diversities of it are largely painful—which is evoked for us by a master who has already proved himself to be one of the greatest of novelists. The end is defeat, or what looks like final disaster.

The chapter in which Ursula has to contemplate this, and her own 'nullity'—it is the concluding chapter of the book—has for title 'The Rainbow'. It begins: 'Ursula went home to Beldover', and ends with the symbolic rainbow. 'She could scarcely speak or notice' when she came home, and 'the weeks crawled by'. On a listless walk by herself, she suffers the pathological nightmare of the horses, staggers home, and collapses into bed. It is convalescing in her bedroom that, at the window, she has her rainbow vision. The final paragraph of the book closes: 'She saw in the rainbow the earth's new architecture, the old, brittle corruption of houses and factories swept away, the world built up in a living fabric of Truth, fitting to the overarching heavens.'

This is indeed quasi-hope—undaunted faith—overhung by dark menace. For we certainly have to take it as, in a way, endorsed by Lawrence himself: there can be no irony. The paradox I point to with my 'quasi-hope' and 'faith' is there in the opening chapter. Lawrence doesn't for one moment let us suppose that, in sum, he would have wished to preserve, if he could, the old Brangwen civilization ('We've been here above *two* hundred years', he tells the Polish lady when courting). The marriage of Tom Brangwen to Lydia Lensky furthered the development that led to the East-wood in which Lawrence was born. In the old rural civilization the lively intellectual milieu in which Lawrence formed and nour-ished his genius wouldn't have been possible. Yet Eastwood was a characteristic product of that developing civilization regarding which he was so sure that, of its very nature, it was heading to the most final of disasters. The paradox was the life in him which perceived, and fought against, the irreversible drive, the lethal upshot of which seemed certain, and at the same time cherished the certitude that life would refuse ever to suffer final defeat. The Laurentian rainbow of the title was the assurance.

The novel ends on Ursula's rainbow vision; but there is no rainbow in the sequel. There could hardly be; the communication of *Women in Love* is, in its Laurentian cogency, too complete.

Was this then all that remained? Was there left nothing but to break off from the happy creative being, was the time up—Is our day of creative life finished?

I have quoted these questions before; they form part of Birkin's brooding, in the chapter where he throws stones to disperse the reflected moon in the millpond, over the inevitable disaster towards which our civilization is taking us. When, at the end of *Women in Love*, he comes back with Ursula from Verona to see to Gerald's frozen corpse, it is as if the answer to those questions were given: 'Yes.' Birkin's earlier apprehensions—by which he 'was frightened'—were justified.

No rainbow, then. Yet Ursula was with him, and there is every sign that the problem of marriage was, for them, solved—solved permanently. This is the point at which to emphasize the title that Lawrence chose for his novel. It reminds one for how much, where Lawrence was concerned, the relations between woman and man counted in any question regarding the livingness of a culture, the health of a civilization. Where the habit, economy and institutional ethos of a civilization should tend to make proper relations—relations involving recognition of the total difference between them and of the nature of their essential need of each other—impossible, there could be, Lawrence clearly believed, little livingness and no hope.

It would be a delicate and exacting business holding forth on the relative significance of Gerald's ominous death on the one hand and of the felicitous mating between Ursula and Birkin on the other—the significances, that is, weighed against one another in their bearing on the effect of the total novel. But what there was of paradox in the book was inescapable in the nature of the enterprise it represented. You could hardly expose the nature of the unsuccess of the one pair without creating a successful pair as a kind of norm—at any rate, if you were Lawrence. He wouldn't have committed himself to the inquest into civilization in England if he hadn't been the gifted being who said, 'Nothing is important but life.' Thus *Women in Love* is paradoxically an affirmation; to serve life is the implicit and inseparable intention, the very spirit, of the creativity that produced it. It couldn't accommodate an equivalent of the rainbow passage with which Ursula concludes *The Rainbow*; but that Lawrence wrote *The Rainbow* and insisted that *Women in Love* was the sequel has a clear significance.

Women in Love is a great novel, and a peculiarly important one. By 'important' I mean that, read and understood, it could have begun the reversal of the process by which, in Lawrence's time, the educated public was being destroyed. But a pretty vain hypothesis is involved in my saying that. The thought necessary to the discrediting of the assumptions behind the civilization that is diagnosed in Lawrence's novel was so original, so unfamiliar that it met with general blankness; its cogency was unperceived. The assumptions themselves made readers blind to the thought. Nevertheless, some few would have been impressed by the force of it; and, in the course of time, a larger minority would have learnt to understand it. And that minority might have determined the attitude of an influential educated public—had there been one.

But already by 1930, the year of Lawrence's death, there wasn't an influential educated reading public; such a public had disappeared. The great change precipitated by the war of 1914 had by then become shockingly obvious—at any rate, to intelligent readers. For naturally, there still were intelligent readers; but there was no organ where they could count on finding intelligent criticism. Certainly they would have looked in vain for evidence that the current critical function was anywhere in contemporary England being responsibly performed. If there had been a reading public both intelligent about literature and influential, would the success of the Faber and Faber 'Poetical Renascence' have been possible? Would the exaltation of Auden into a major poet have been so unembarrassed by outspoken critical resistance? Would Faber and Faber's advertising manager have thought it worth while to let Spender be called, in the publicity of the firm, 'the Shelley of this Poetical Renascence'? The literary world had been made—and was kept—safe for these coterie valuations, for the coterie controlled the literary world; it *was* it. In *The New Statesman* (while it mattered), *The Times Literary Supplement* and the Sunday papers, the stalwarts of the coterie and its recruits have enjoyed for decades now a monopoly of the literary reviewing. Naturally they use it in a coterie spirit, which—naturally, too—is determined to maintain the coterie privilege (which is necessarily anti-critical).

Lawrence remarked half-a-century ago that the passion for equality was now the only religion left. The 'passion for equality' is the religion of egalitarianism; and no one more or less grown up expects the religion you profess and the life you actually lead to be wholly consistent with one another: the advanced development of democracy we have achieved in this country has brought home to us that unqualified equality is hard to establish, and would be, even if we restricted the ideal to terms of money, power and privilege. Even left-wing extremists know that you can't do without differentials; Mr Benn himself knows that you have to have statesmen—that is, politicians who have authority, power and opportunity, and don't shrink from using them to face the electorate with *faits accomplis*; and with the advance of our democracy, bureaucrats multiply.

Nevertheless, the ubiquity of egalitarianism as the modern 'religion' means that few people seem to be disturbed at the supreme anti-human triumph of the technologico-Benthamite spirit: the proclaimed (and enforceable) 'equality' of women and men; whereas difference is the essential fact, and it is not a matter of inequality or 'underprivilege'; difference, without which there could be no completely human humanity. Well, this can be dispensed with, though difference will perversely remain; it can by no means be completely abolished, merely impoverished, frustrated and perverted—effects which our democratic civilization ensures. The destructive influence of egalitarianism on education is possibly less frightening in its enmity to life; nevertheless, it *is* radically destructive. One would find, however, strong support in opposing it, and it is sometimes possible to oppose it without being grossly misunderstood.

A distinctive characteristic of democratic civilization four or five decades after Lawrence's death is that we now have a Minister for the Arts balancing a Minister for Sport. The pretty general sense that this duality of governmental concern evinces a healthy impartiality is depressing; but it is a natural manifestation of what our civilization is. The Minister for the Arts has set up an Arts Council, which in pursuance of its business of fostering creative productivity can draw on public funds (that is, on the taxpayer's pocket). It was in *The Times Literary Supplement* that I learnt that the Arts Council was contributing some thousands of pounds in order to make possible the successful launching and establishment of *The New Review*, edited by Mr Ian Hamilton. All the signs are that Mr Hamilton, having had some connection (at least as a contributor), is on intimate terms with Mr John Gross, the editor of *The Times Literary Supplement*. And not long after reading the paragraph in *The Times Literary Supplement* I received a circular announcing the foundation of 'The New Fiction Society', 'an important new scheme to promote fiction in Britain', launched by 'the Arts Council, in association with the National Book League.'

'The aim of The New Fiction Society is to encourage interest in new and established writers. It will do this by the publicity and sales it secures for their novels; and by enabling publishers substantially to increase their print runs – thus bringing down the price of good new novels.'

The unknown responsible for the choice of books is 'assisted by an advisory panel' consisting of the Literary Editor of *The New Statesman*, the former Literary Editor of *The Times* (now 'its senior book reviewer'), and Professor Kermode, former chairman of the Arts Council Literature Panel. The books chosen 'are all personally signed by the authors'. 'Each of these famous writers has chosen his or her favourite of their own novels.' The first name on the list of the lucky famous writers favoured this year (1975) is Kingsley Amis.

The Arts Council, then, where the literary product is in question, is the reliable instrument of the 'Literary World', the 'world' that has a virtual monopoly of the literary reviewing, so that its consensus establishes who the important contemporary writers are, and ensures them the possibility of living by their pens (a ridiculously minimal statement, of course, when applied to Kingsley Amis—and a good many others).

When the 'transvaluation of values' has attained to this completeness, the educated public, the public in whom 'standards' reside, has beyond question been eliminated. Of course, there are grave consequences for literature, creativity and mankind. When, recently, Mr John Gross approached me with the urbane suggestion that, much as I might disapprove of *The Times Literary Supplement*, I would naturally let him add my signature to the letter of protest that was about to appear in it against the compulsory unionization of journalists, I answered 'No.' The reason I gave him was that the policy pursued for some decades by *The Times Literary Supplement* had done more damage to civilization than the proposed legal measure would do. (Another reason was implicit in the form I gave, in the close of my reply, to my repeated and reinforced refusal: 'I will not allow you to use my name in the way you propose.' (When the letter of protest appeared in print the suspicion I had intimated was confirmed by the list of signatories to which my name would have been added.)

To destroy the educated public is to kill English literature—past literature as a living influence, and the possibility of significant new creation in the present. This is what the predecessors of Mr John Gross and his friends had done, and they themselves take the opportunities of profit, privilege, and power (which includes the power to suppress) they inherit. There is no mystery about the barrenness of the period since the beginning of the last war, when Eliot completed 'Little Gidding' and gave up poetry: actually, one can say, there has been nothing that told as new life since Lawrence died, and Eliot, as major poet, was 'superseded' by Auden. In any case, the poetry of Eliot's that was influential belonged to the 1920s—and what earned him the O.M. wasn't his genius.

What chance had potential creative originality of developing after 1930? There was no *English Review*. Even before the Great War Ford succeeded in keeping his *English Review—The English Review* that mattered—going for only a very few years. Without Ford and the organ he controlled, even Lawrence, the prodigiously gifted, must have had a much more difficult start. And the lively milieu he created at Eastwood, and needed for his development, couldn't have been created if there hadn't been an influential cultivated public—a public which expected intelligent reviews and informed criticism in the newspapers and weeklies it read. Without the stimulus and information derived from such sources no provincial group could have attained to the intellectual culture that astonished Ford.

In these days of the Arts Council and Reg Prentices as Ministers of Education, creative gifts, however charged with potentiality, don't develop. Lawrence would hardly have been surprised at the so much more effectual hostility to creative livingness shown to life by civilization in our time. But would there, in face of the present overt menace reflected in every day's newspaper, have been any hint of a rainbow in a Laurentian constatation of a catastrophe that was certain to finish off our civilization? 'It is no use trying merely to modify present forms. The whole great form of our era will have to go.' I think he was right; but if one had adjusted oneself to his thought, fifty years ago, well enough to say that, there would have been something theoretical about one's endorsement. Lawrence meant with full conviction what he said—and yet, as we have noted, there is an element of 'paradoxical' faith—irrepressible life-assertion—in the context: 'And one can do nothing, but fight tooth and nail to defend the new shoots of life from being crushed out, and let them grow.' Would he have been able to imply so confidently that, *after* the catastrophe that hangs over us, new shoots of life will spring up, and slowly burst through the foundations (and the rubble)—life representing promise and hope? But it is pointless to ask that; Lawrence died in 1930, and, in the changed world of today, he would have been ninety. What we know is that the Laurentian genius, as we have it, is convincing—is irresistible. The tribute we pay it is to know that the naïve rainbow-symbol as he subtilized it, making it paradoxical, is valid for us. When I say 'we' I mean those who have recognized in his a voice pre-eminently demanding our attention and found the clear truth he conveys truth to live with and to ponder. I am conscious, too, of assuming that they share my conviction as to the effort we have to make. The nature of that conviction is defined briefly in the third epigraph (the one I wrote myself) to my last book: *The Living Principle: 'English' as a Discipline of Thought*. I will quote three sentences from it here:

If you believe in humanity at all you will know that nothing today is more important than to keep alive the idea of the university function—the essential university-function and what goes with it: the idea of an educated public. My preoccupation is to ensure that the living seed exists, and that the life in it has the full pregnancy. Just how it will strike and take and develop, as it *must* if there is to be a human future, one can't foresee.'

Why I associate so intimately the conviction and the effort with Lawrence I have made plain, I hope, in the present book. The associating is the way that the change since Lawrence's time imposes on me of invoking his paradoxical rainbow—of daring to postulate that human life will go on. I felt the courage grow in me as I met more and more people who shared my conviction about him and the nature of his genius: he has readers who understand him. I now see grounds for believing that they begin to form a public, and that we should be thinking about the ways of making it more effectively and consciously a public. It is in numbers very small, and, at its largest, will inevitably remain numerically very small. But influence is not a matter of numerical impressiveness. Civilization's belief in what it stands for has broken down, and humanity has a desperate sense of the vacuum. Lawrence even in that prefatory Note is expressing a belief that compels him to communicate his insight and his rationality. He is himself a force of life bursting through the hard surface. As he implicitly tells us, we too are life.

VI

FURTHER CONSIDERATIONS

LAWRENCE'S perspicacity about the future followed from his insight into the present. Between the Armistice and his death the change he witnessed made it plain that the consequences of the war couldn't be reversed; the reinforced drive of civilization was invincible.[1] I have said, then, that he wouldn't have been surprised at anything in today's England. Yet to foresee is not the same as experiencing the actuality. And so there is a sense in which the present-day actuality couldn't really be anticipated— even in 1930, when the utterly undistinguished Kingsley Martin became an intellectual power in England; to be matched, a little later, by Auden as a major poet.

These were my reflections when, in P. T. Bauer's *Dissent on Development*, I came on what I will in a moment quote. I am grateful to Bauer; it is his virtues and intellectual distinction that make him worth quoting. The book is an honest, lucid exposure by a trained economist, who is both intelligent and well-informed, of the fallacies, falsities, dishonesties, contradictions and nonsensicalities that form the staple of what passes for discussion of the alleged duty of the 'developed countries' to give generous 'aid' to the 'underdeveloped'. He is led by the stylistic habits and ostensible thinking of economists, and above all by the shamelessly unscrupulous use of terms that purport to be precise, having been fitted for strict use in 'social science' by careful definition, to write this[2]:

This debasement of language undermines effective communication, on which the reasonably smooth functioning of civilized society largely depends. Words are to communication and discussion what units of currency are to a monetary system. The debasement of language, as of money, must promote disintegration.

Bauer, of course, is an economist; but he is an intelligent one,

[1] 'Between Lloyd George and Rufus Isaacs, etc., we are done—you asked me a year ago who won the war—we've all lost it.'
         Letters, p. 546. To Lady Cynthia Asquith, 30th April, 1922.
[2] *Dissent on Development*, p. 322.

147

and intensely concerned for the standards that make fruitful discussion and disciplined thought, in the field of his study, possible.
What is more, he has a firm grasp of the truth that economics,
however indispensable in our civilization, can't at best be strictly a
science. It is his virtues, as I have said, that make the notion of
language to which he commits himself so significant. For it is not
possible to suppose that he confines his meaning to language as
used in economics; the last sentence of my brief quotation makes
that plain.

It is obvious enough that the parallel between debased language
and debased currency is general in intention. But a society held
together by communication in a language describable as being of
words that are the equivalents of a currency is unimaginable. In
fact, the offered parallel of a language and a monetary currency
is profoundly revealing; it exposes the desperate plight of our
civilization, for Bauer is a notably intelligent man. There may be
some indelicacy, I am afraid in my actually making the point I
had in mind when I quoted those sentences. But it is this: there
is one sufficiently representative thing I can say towards defining
my 'educated public': its members would be persons both capable
of appreciating the distinction and value of Bauer's book, and at
the same time capable of seeing at once why the quoted passage
is absurd. Its presence in so distinguished a book is a sign that there
is now no 'educated public'; and the lack of one is a grave disability for a thinker of that quality. But we live in an age when
Lord Robbins, planning a revolutionary advance in Higher
Education, relied on Psychology and Social Science for humane
supplementation to the stricter sciences.

Lawrence beyond question saw the menace of this development,
but it is a great change. And with the disappearance of the educated public, the country's memory fails; what has lapsed is lost—
it ceases to live as memory. What *is* England? one asks. I was
prompted to ask it by coming on this in the *Letters*—it was written
in the spring of 1922:

But I do think, still more now I am out here, that we made a mistake
forsaking England and moving out into the periphery of life. After all,
Taormina, Ceylon, Africa, America—as far as *we* go, they are only
the negation of what we stand for and are: and we're rather like Jonahs
running away from the place we belong. ... I really think that the

most living clue of life is in us Englishmen in England, and the great
mistake we make is in not uniting together in the strength of the real
living clue—religious in the most vital sense—uniting together in
England, and so carrying the vital spark through. Because so far as we are
concerned it is in danger of being quenched. I know now it is a shirk-
ing of the issue to look to Buddha or the Hindu or to our own working
men for the impulse to carry through. It is in ourselves, or nowhere
and this looking to the outer masses is only a betrayal.[1]

A little later in the same spring he writes to Lady Cynthia Asquith:[2]

I break my heart over England when I am out here. Those natives
are *back* of us—in the living sense *lower* than we are. But they are going
to swarm over us and suffocate us. We are, have been for five centuries,
the growing tip. Now we're going to fall. But you don't catch me
going back on my whiteness and Englishness and myself. English in
the teeth of all the world, even in the teeth of England. How England
deliberately undermines England.

No one at all could write like this now. Such things—and the note
is common in Lawrence—bring home to us that England exists no
longer. The politicians and leader-writers and voices from the
BBC, when they talk of national recovery and of restoring
England's prestige, are thinking only of economic recovery and
of the prestige of a rising growth-rate. I have commented in a
previous book on the significance of the full-page advertisement
that, when the issue was still in doubt, appeared in *The Times* and
other papers: 'Joining Europe means more jobs in this country.'
Just that. And we joined. And the promoters of our 'going
European' will be triumphant if the calculation works out so,
the promise is fulfilled, and there ultimately *are*.

Some powerful interest, with firm convictions and access to
funds, paid for that expensive advertisement. There is no need to
impute any illegitimate motivation; but no doubt behind the
subsidy there was reasonable certitude among the subsidizers that
they themselves stood to profit by a 'Yes' vote in the referendum.
They were justified in their assumption that what they had to
make sure of defeating was xenophobia-cum-conservatism: any
genuine cultural solicitude in the electorate was negligible; the
effective appeal would be to material self-interest, and the drafter
of the advertisement chose cannily.

[1] *Letters* (Aldous Huxley's collection), p. 542.   [2] Ibid., p. 546.

THOUGHT, WORDS AND CREATIVITY

This is the first significance of that well-timed advertisement together with the victory of the E.E.C. But the advertisement itself is memorable in another way; it represents the decisive victory of 'job' over 'to be not unemployed'; to be unemployed now is to be 'jobless', and the state one is in is 'joblessness', which is personal unemployment. The change is endorsed even by *The Times*, and even on its leader-page. Rightly considered, it is a portentous change—one not, so far as I am aware, allowed for, at any rate explicitly, by Lawrence, so that it affects at least the expression of his wisdom about 'work'.

I remember Bloomsbury's senior critic, sage and wit, the late Desmond MacCarthy, coming out with the flash of insight that Lawrence's great affinity was Carlyle. Well, it is true that Carlyle was in his time the great enemy of Benthamism and a staunch unbeliever in progress. Perhaps (though I can't believe that there were ever any such) there are living witnesses who can testify to a weakness in Lawrence for Frederick the Great. The simplest way of disposing of MacCarthy's *aperçu* is to recall that Carlyle stood, with characteristic sour gloom about life and humanity, for the 'gospel of work'. No basic attitude could be more anti-Laurentian. This is made explicit in that early long 'Study of Thomas Hardy' which he never published (it is a preliminary sustained self-exploration, carried out arduously and comprehensively, to establish for himself what he believes and where he stands).

I will be parsimonious in my quoting, the paperback is to hand, and the context of this brief passage is readily accessible[1]:

This is the glamour of kings, the glamour of men who had the opportunity to *be*, who were not under compulsion to do, to serve. This is why kings were chosen heroes, because they were the beings, the producers of new life, not servants of necessity, repeating old experience.

And humanity has laboured to make work shorter, so we may all be kings. True, we have the necessity to work, more or less, according as we are near the growing tip, or further away. Some men are far from the growing tip. They have little for growth in them, only the power for repeating old movement. They will always find their own level. But let those that have life, live.

[1] The paperback was extracted from *Phoenix I* by Mr J. V. Davies. The passage begins at the last word on p. 38 (paperback) and p. 425 (*Phoenix*).

So there has been produced machinery, to take the place of the human machine. And the inventor of the labour-saving machine has been hailed as a public benefactor, and we have rejoiced over his discovery. Now there is a railing against the machine, as if it were an evil thing. And the thinkers talk about the return to the medieval system of handicrafts. Which is absurd.

★   ★   ★

Wherefore I do honour to the machine and to its inventor.

But 'jobless' and 'joblessness'—why does the established contemporary use of the word 'job' mean that there has been a revolutionary change? Everyone knows the answer: the worker is now on top, every worker has a claim to a job, and the claim to a job defines a 'worker'. He is safe against being sweated (his claim to a job means, in any case, a claim to a 'living wage'). Nevertheless, he is genuinely and grievously a victim of our civilization, though he himself together with his formidably armed guardians is unaware of it. His grievances are all material: 'Money on the table!'

We are driven to recognize that Lawrence's distinction between the necessity of work and the opportunity to *be* involves an oversimplification. The worker nowadays has his leisure right enough, but discovers—or mostly doesn't discover—that to *be* is a positive art that he hasn't begun to learn and has no chance of learning.

The 'mostly' in my last sentence allows for this consideration of Lawrence's in the passage I quote above:

> Some men are far from the growing tip. They have little for growth in them, only the power for repeating old movement. They will always find their own level. But let those who have life, live.

I am forced to say again that this too is not a possible attitude today. Work in Lawrence's own life was represented by teaching in an elementary school. He was able to give it up, and not to commit himself to other 'work', because he was so wonderfully gifted and because England was then a country in which Ford could conceive and run his *English Review*. True, its life was short —the coming war killed it; but it couldn't have existed at all if there hadn't been an educated public and a living English literature. Lawrence's gifts were of a kind that entailed his never ceasing to *be*, and ensured a prodigious expenditure of energy in his intensities of *being*. His art, his quest of articulateness and consciousness, sharpened and sensitized his living, and his living nourished his art.

Persons of Lawrence's kind of gift are rare, but they are centres of radiant potency—of life that irradiates people in whom the creativity is less powerful. Lawrence intimates their importance to the age in his 'more or less, according as we are near the growing tip, or further away'. He *was* the growing tip; which means that his genius in its transcendence was so much more than his individual self: in him the élite that kept the language living found, in being sensitized by the genius, and responsive to it, the living tip of the language.

But all this, in the age of Social Studies, is incomprehensible nonsense. The workers now have leisure, but that doesn't bring with it the power to be. It doesn't exist in the world where there is no growing tip. And what Lawrence says—to quote it again for the sake of the immediate point—in *Mornings in Mexico* of the Indians is very relevant:

They are all involved at every moment in their old, struggling religion.

Until they break in a kind of hopelessness ... Which is what is rapidly happening. The young Indians who have been to school for many years are losing their religion, becoming discontented, bored and rootless. An Indian with his own religion inside him *cannot* be bored. The flow of the mytery is too intense all the time.

An implicit intimation that, in Lawrence's judgment, a certain boredom characterized technologico-Benthamite civilization in his time is detectable here. Until the other day one would have expected the comment that, in our time, when democracy has been pretty completely attained, but is still advancing, boredom is unquestionably a mark of our civilized 'way of life'—a comment to be met confidently with: Boredom?—how can a population be bored when all the talents and resources (including colour-television) at the disposal of the BBC are professionally marshalled to ensure that no one need spend a vacuous hour?

But the change from Lawrence's England—a major change that can't be disputed—is that no one today would refer to 'our cheerful, triumphant success'. The hopelessness is ours. It is ostensibly so justified that the possibility of a long-deferred but ultimately regained steady growth-rate may, for a while, seem a vitalizing hope—something spiritual.

Before I close I should say something more about the suggestion that, in the way he distinguishes between 'work' and the concern 'to be', Lawrence oversimplifies. I have already pointed to the fact that, in 'being', he himself incurred an endless expenditure of energy, directed and undirected—my 'undirected' is a recognition that his power of spontaneous interest (which was itself creative) was always growing and always open to the new. And I have tried briefly to suggest how, in a vital culture, the potency that inhered in such giftedness as his made, *via* more ordinary people, an essential difference to society as a whole.

Lawrence doesn't simplify in his art. It was still possible in his time to assume unquestioningly that 'more ordinary people' kept alive the cultural tradition that made the rare important artist himself, the growing tip, the decisively major creativity, possible. I will take my illustration from 'The Fox', which is one of his supreme *nouvelles*. There is the introductory conversation between the girls who are running the little farm together and the young soldier who had lived there before the war, and who, expecting to find his grandfather, had broken in on them.

He was very curious about the girls, to find out exactly what they were doing. His questions were those of a farm youth; acute, practical, a little mocking. He was very much amused by their attitude to their losses: for they were amusing on the score of heifers and fowls.

'Oh well,' broke in March, 'we don't believe in living for nothing but work.'

'Don't you?' he answered. And again the quick young laugh came over his face. He kept his eyes steadily on the obscure woman in the corner.

The question, 'What for—what ultimately for?', has come up, and it involves, as the continued conversation testifies, not only the relation of work to the concern for 'being', but the difference between woman and man and the mutual need of the one for the other.

'But what will you do when you've used up all your capital?' he said.

'Oh, I don't know,' answered March laconically.

'Hire ourselves out for land-workers, I suppose.'

'Yes, but there won't be any demand for women land-workers now that the war's over,' said the youth.

'Oh, we'll see. We shall hold on a bit longer yet,' said March, with a plangent, half-sad, half-ironical indifference.

'There wants a man about the place,' said the youth softly.

Banford burst out laughing.

'Take care what you say,' she interrupted. 'We consider ourselves quite efficient.'

'Oh,' came March's slow plangent voice, 'it isn't a case of efficiency, I'm afraid. If you're going to do farming you must be at it from morning till night, and you might as well be a beast yourself.'

'Yes, that's it,' said the youth. 'You aren't willing to put yourselves into it.'

'We aren't,' said March, 'and we know it.'

'We want some of our time for ourselves,' said Banford.

The youth threw himself back on the sofa, his face tight with laughter, and laughed silently, but thoroughly. The calm scorn of the girls tickled him tremendously.

Henry's whole attitude makes it plain that *he* sees nothing against being 'willing to put yourself into it'—except that March and Banford are women, and 'There wants a man about the place.' He is characterized by Lawrence as a hunter, but, in his practical spirit, he imagines himself married to March and running the place, and *we* can imagine him too. It is plain that, for him, it wouldn't be 'work' as opposed to living, but both at the same time; and to such living in a less ordinary person we shouldn't hesitate to apply Lawrence's verb and say that, for Henry, to have work that he willingly 'gives himself to' is to be.

It is beyond question that he is strongly attracted to March; he proposes and is not rejected. Lawrence's judgment is clear: March's devoting herself to the ailing and non-marrying Jill is against nature, and can't make either happy.

Poor March, in her goodwill and her responsibility, she had strained herself till it seemed to her that the whole of life and everything was only a horrible gulf of nothingness.

Stating his profound conviction, Lawrence resorts again to the rainbow-symbol, which—for once—he uses to express an intensity of negation:

And women? What goal can any woman conceive, except happiness? Just happiness, for herself and the whole world. That, and nothing else. And so, she assumes the responsibility, and sets off towards her goal. She can see it there, at the foot of the rainbow. Or she can see it a little way beyond, in the blue distance. Not far, not far.

But the end of the rainbow is a bottomless gulf down which you can fall forever without arriving, and the blue distance is a void pit which can swallow you and all your efforts into its emptiness, and still be no emptier. You and all your efforts. So the illusion of attainable happiness.

Poor March, she had set off so wonderfully towards the blue goal. And the further and further she had gone, the more fearful had become the realization of emptiness. An agony, an insanity at last.

She was glad it was over. She was glad to sit on the shore and look westward over the sea, and know that the great strain had ended. She would never strain for love and happiness any more. And Jill was safely dead. Poor Jill, poor Jill. It must be sweet to be safely dead.

For her own part, death was not her destiny. She would have to leave her destiny to the boy.

Of course this has a context. But the end of 'The Fox' (which is not far away from it) is comparable in significance to the successful close of Birkin's courtship of Ursula. Birkin is cultivated, and very much more articulate and intellectual than 'the boy'; if he isn't, like Lawrence, the growing tip itself, he is—as the boy is not—fully aware that there *is*, or ought to be, one, and his uncompromising concern for it gives the significance to his life that he can't do without. That is, he is in his individuality 'created' and self-responsible, which is inseparable from his recognizing his basic responsibility in relation to life—to the life-issue.

Henry Grenfell and March aren't 'in love' with one another, but they feel, in their necessarily different ways, a strong mutual attraction. For March, 'there is such rest in the boy': he has saved her from the emptiness at the foot of the rainbow—from her vain self-dedication to making Jill happy and from supposing that aim capable of injecting significance into life.

Mutual need is also a problem. Henry needs, on his side, her. The problem isn't solved easily; the strain in her resulting from her long-drawn-out and despairing struggle doesn't yield at once. But the 'undercurrent' in him knows—and the whole context bears him out—that the yielding will finally come.

He chafed, feeling that he hadn't got his own life. He would never have it till she yielded and slept in him. Then he would have all his own life as a young man and a mate, and she would have all her own life as a woman and a female. There would be no more of this awful straining. She would not be a man any more, an independent woman with a man's responsibility.

What is expressed here—and it is dramatically presented in the novel—is the vital true relation between man and woman as Lawrence conceived it. It is the pattern of what is fully articulate in Birkin, whose insight is ultimately endorsed by Ursula, the troubled but sternly adverse critic of Skrebensky; not inequality, but difference—difference that is essential to life. And the essentialness isn't merely biological. Lawrence insists on this dramatically and unanswerably; the explicitness in the close is subsequent, underlining what has been *done*.

Henry couldn't have been articulate as Lawrence's art enables *him* to be on Henry's behalf. But Birkin's explicitness, addressed to Ursula, is convincingly dramatic as *his*. For whereas Henry and March are ordinary, both Birkin and Ursula are gifted and unusual. But the Laurentian insistence is always on individuality—on the need to 'single' oneself and be oneself, whether one is a woman or a man. He puts it explicitly in such statements as this: 'That she bear children is not a woman's significance. But that she bear herself, that is her supreme and risky fate.'

The living cultural tradition that made 'The Fox' possible in 'art-speech' has been destroyed. I have suggested that this is the gravest, most anti-human aspect of the change since Lawrence died. A new Lawrence has certainly been made impossible by the changed conditions; and it is obviously nonsensical to ask whether he could have held to his indestructible life-courage had he been alive today. His religious intuition of the primacy of life was such that he was capable of saying that even if human life extinguished itself, or was eliminated from the world, new life would be generated in the universe. That faith was possible for a Lawrence in *his* time, but we, in the present age, can hardly share it, nor would it comfort us if we could. But we have the incitement, which is irresistible, of the life-courage in the product of his creativity, and that makes it inevitable for us to carry on the creative effort with all our intelligence, courage and resource. Who can be sure? Logic and automatism, impossible as it now seems, may yet be robbed of their final victory; the decisively new and unforeseen may yet reward us.